The Conscious Choice

Bhavna Toor is the founder and CEO of Shenomics, dedicated to accelerating inclusive leadership with wisdom and compassion. A globally recognized expert in conscious leadership, she has trained and coached high-potential leaders at over 250 leading organizations and helped accelerate the careers of 1,00,000+ professionals worldwide.

A TEDx speaker and LinkedIn Top Voice for Gender Equity, Bhavna has been featured in *People Matters, Economic Times* and *Thrive Global*. She holds an MBA from NYU Stern and has received multiple accolades, including Global Women of Influence 2024.

She is the co-founder of the Lead Like a Girl Global Foundation and the creator of the Lead Like a Girl Fellowship, empowering aspiring women leaders across Asia and Africa.

A former Miss India New York and host of *The Conscious Woman Podcast*, Bhavna is a passionate advocate for compassionate workplaces.

A true global citizen, she has lived in eight countries, including the US, UK, Nigeria, India and now Singapore, and brings a global perspective to her work. Learn more at shenomics.com.

Praise for *The Conscious Choice*

'Bhavna Toor's book is a thought-provoking guide to live your life with more mindfulness. A brilliant read – brought alive through her simple yet powerful personal anecdotes!'

Geetika Mehta, Managing Director, Nivea India, *ET* 40 Under 40

'*The Conscious Choice* is a gem. [Toor's] genius lies in the value she packs into each short chapter and the questions she poses … If you ruminate on the questions, answer them honestly and act on the ideas that come to you, your experience of life will change – profoundly and for the better. Keep this book lying around. Thumb through it at odd times and read random chapters. You will benefit greatly'

Dr Srikumar Rao, founder of The Rao Institute and author of *Modern Wisdom, Ancient Roots*

'*The Conscious Choice* is a transformative guide to conscious leadership … profound insights and practical wisdom make this book a must-read for anyone seeking to lead with intention and empathy'

Veda Persad, Country Executive, Northern Trust Corporation

'[This] insightful book is a powerful reminder that our daily choices, made consciously, hold the key to creating a life filled with clarity, purpose and genuine fulfillment'

Dorie Clark, professor, Columbia Business School and author of *The Long Game*

'Reading *The Conscious Choice* felt like having a heart-to-heart with a wise friend – one who gently reminds you of your power to shape your life, one choice at a time. Highly recommended!'

Mette Johansson, author of *Narratives: the Stories that Hold Women Back at Work*

'Bhavna's great storytelling makes it very easy to just pick a choice and dive in, to live more mindfully'

Dalia Feldheim, author of *Lead Like a Girl*

The Conscious Choice

100 Ideas for
Living and Leading Mindfully

BHAVNA TOOR

Illustrated by Meghna Menon

PAN

First published 2025 by Pan
an imprint of Pan Macmillan Publishing India Private Limited
707 Kailash Building
26 K. G. Marg, New Delhi 110001
www.panmacmillan.co.in

Pan Macmillan, The Smithson, 6 Briset Street, Farringdon, London EC1M 5NR
Associated companies throughout the world
www.panmacmillan.com

ISBN 978-93-6113-115-8

Copyright © Bhavna Toor 2025

Illustrations by Meghna Menon

The moral rights of the author have been asserted.

The views expressed in this book are the author's own and the facts reported by them have been verified by the publisher to the extent possible. The publisher hereby disclaims any liability to any party for loss, damages or disruptions caused by the same.

All rights reserved. No part of this publication may be reproduced, stored in or introduced into a retrieval system, or transmitted, in any form, or by any means (electronic, mechanical, photocopying, recording or otherwise) without the prior written permission of the publisher. Any person who does any unauthorized act in relation to this publication may be liable to criminal prosecution and civil claims for damages.

1 3 5 7 9 8 6 4 2

This book is sold subject to the condition that it shall not, by way of trade or otherwise, be lent, re-sold, hired out, or otherwise circulated without the publisher's prior consent in any form of binding or cover other than that in which it is published and without a similar condition including this condition being imposed on the subsequent purchaser.

Typeset in Petersburg by R. Ajith Kumar, New Delhi
Printed and bound in India by
Thomson Press India Ltd.

To my family:
'I am because we are.'

Contents

Introduction: The Power of Conscious Choice   xiii

1.	Success or Failure?	1
2.	Inside-Out or Outside-In?	4
3.	Fear or Adventure?	7
4.	Possible or Impossible?	10
5.	What or Why?	14
6.	Character or Skill?	17
7.	Open Doors or Close Them?	20
8.	Focus on Actions or Outcomes?	23
9.	Feedback or Feed-forward?	26
10.	Static Opinions or Working Hypotheses?	29
11.	Schadenfreude or Freudenfreude?	32
12.	Self-Judgment or Self-Awareness?	35
13.	I Don't or I Can't?	38
14.	Step In or Step Back?	40
15.	Purpose or Passion?	43
16.	Addition or Subtraction?	46
17.	Raise the Bar or Lower It?	49
18.	Pull Out the Thorn or Live Around It?	52
19.	Delayed Gratification or Ever-Present Gratification?	56

20.	To Fall or To Rise Stronger?	60
21.	The First or the Second Arrow?	63
22.	The Bud or the Flower?	66
23.	Day One or Day Two?	69
24.	Press Record or Fast-Forward?	71
25.	Avoid Boredom or Love It?	74
26.	The Beginner's Mind or the Expert Mind?	77
27.	Do It Fearlessly or Do It Afraid?	80
28.	Overcome Impostor Syndrome or Celebrate It?	83
29.	Desire A or Desire B?	86
30.	Zoom In or Zoom Out?	89
31.	Be Direct or Set High Expectations?	92
32.	Lay Bricks or Build a Cathedral?	95
33.	Human Doing or Human Being?	98
34.	Procrastination or Progress?	101
35.	React or Respond?	104
36.	Positive Thinking or Negative Thinking?	107
37.	Safety or Punishment?	110
38.	Be Yourself or Be Your Best Self?	114
39.	Velcro or Teflon?	117
40.	Scarcity or Abundance?	120
41.	Fierce or Tender Self-Compassion?	124
42.	Remember Life or Remember Death?	128
43.	Darkness or Light?	131
44.	Wait for Good Weather or Dance in the Rain?	135
45.	City A or City B?	138
46.	Be Normal or Embrace Eccentricity?	141
47.	To Give or To Take?	144
48.	Give In or Keep Going?	147
49.	Change Outcome or Change Identity?	150
50.	Your Immediate Circle or Your Wider Circle?	154

Contents

51.	Can't or Won't?	157
52.	Choosing Fun or Waiting for It?	160
53.	Regret as Pain or Self-Awareness?	163
54.	Good or Bad?	166
55.	Fly High or Play Safe?	169
56.	Judgmental or Dispassionate?	172
57.	Student or Teacher?	175
58.	The Bonsai or the Mighty Oak?	178
59.	Pain or Uncertainty?	180
60.	Confidence or Trust?	183
61.	Confidence or Courage?	186
62.	Alone or Together?	189
63.	Turn Toward or Turn Away?	192
64.	Think More or Think Less?	196
65.	Success or People?	199
66.	Lucky or Unlucky?	202
67.	Tear Yourself Down or Build Yourself Up?	205
68.	Open Loops or Closed Loops?	208
69.	Have To or Get To?	211
70.	Past or Future?	214
71.	A Downward Spiral or an Upward Spiral?	217
72.	Avoid Being Wrong or Find Joy In It?	221
73.	Less or More?	224
74.	Fact or Story?	227
75.	The Pebble or the Bridge?	230
76.	Discomfort or Resentment?	233
77.	Contamination or Redemption?	236
78.	Decision or Sacrifice?	239
79.	Good Thing or Bad Thing?	242
80.	Here or There?	245
81.	The Easy Life or a Life of Growth?	249

82.	Ahead or Behind?	253
83.	Quantity or Quality?	256
84.	Autotelic or Exotelic?	260
85.	Quit or Persevere?	263
86.	Time-Poor or Time-Rich?	267
87.	Inner Critic or Inner Coach?	270
88.	A Speck of Dust or a Ripple Through Time?	273
89.	Yes or No?	276
90.	Inspiration or Desperation?	279
91.	Carpe Diem or Carpe Punctum?	282
92.	Jim Carrey or Percy Carrey?	285
93.	Empathy or Compassion?	288
94.	Apples or Oranges?	292
95.	The Antelope or the Mouse?	295
96.	To Seek Help or Not?	298
97.	Forecast or Backcast?	301
98.	Encouraging or Critical?	304
99.	Talent or Skill?	307
100.	Start or Restart?	310

Acknowledgements	313
Notes	315

Introduction

The Power of Conscious Choice

Every day, we make countless choices. Some are small, like what to eat for breakfast or which route to take to work. Others shape the trajectory of our lives, like where to live, which career to pursue, whom to love. Many of these decisions happen automatically, without much thought.

But what if we made them with greater awareness?

This book was born from a simple idea: small, conscious choices made consistently create a life of greater clarity, purpose and meaning.

I know this firsthand.

In 2015, I visited Florence, Italy and stood before the Gates of Paradise, a masterpiece by the artist Lorenzo Ghiberti. He dedicated his entire life to creating just two bronze doors – the first set took him twenty years, and the second set another twenty-one.

As I gazed at the intricacy of his work, I had a realization.

I thought of my own life up to that point as my first set of bronze doors – a body of work I was proud of, but one that hadn't always been created with full intention.

I'd recently left my corporate career in New York to

become a social entrepreneur in India. I had discovered the philosophy of mindfulness, and I had found my passion in helping other women live and lead consciously.

As I stood before the doors, I made a decision: The rest of my life would be my next set of bronze doors – crafted with care, purpose and conscious choice.

As I deepened my practice of mindfulness, I became more intentional about the choices I made. And I saw firsthand the powerful impact of those choices – not just in my own life, but in the lives of the scores of women (and men) who have gone through our programmes at Shenomics.

Research in behavioral psychology shows that when we make decisions with awareness, we feel more in control, fulfilled, and aligned with our values.

Neuroscientists have found that the brain's prefrontal cortex, responsible for decision-making, is trainable – meaning that the more we practise conscious choice, the better we become at shaping our lives intentionally.

Yet, most of us make choices on autopilot, influenced by habit, fear or social expectations. The ancient Stoic philosopher Epictetus put it best:

> The chief task in life is simply this: to identify and separate matters so that I can say clearly to myself which are externals not under my control, and which have to do with the choices I actually control.

This book isn't here to tell you which choices to make, but to guide you in making your choices consciously. There is no judgment here – only an invitation to pause, reflect and decide with greater awareness.

Whether you choose empathy or compassion, talent or skill, the antelope or the mouse, the key is to make the choice intentionally. When you do, you'll find yourself more aligned with the life you truly want to live.

There is no set order to reading these chapters. Pick any chapter that speaks to you. Read it, reflect on the question at the end, and apply the insight in your own way.

Some chapters will challenge you. Others will affirm what you already know deep down. But each one is designed to help you make conscious choices that bring you closer to clarity, purpose and fulfillment.

You are just one choice away from a new perspective, a new habit, a new path.

So where do you want to start?

Pick a chapter. Read the question. And let your journey begin.

1

Success or Failure?

On choosing the stories we create

The year was 2010. I was in New York, interviewing for a role with a consulting firm. Like many soon-to-be business school graduates, I thought the logical next step was to follow the herd – to pursue a job in investment banking or consulting.

As I sat in front of the woman interviewing me, I was visibly uneasy. Like I didn't belong, and didn't quite know what I was even doing there. At one point in the interview, she asked me, 'Tell me about a time you failed and what you learned from it.'

I just stared at her, dumbfounded.

You would think this was a standard interview question that I would have prepared for. But I hadn't. My mind went completely blank and I couldn't think of a single failure story that felt genuine enough to share. (Did failing my driving test count?) I fumbled through the rest of the interview and left feeling completely dejected.

That moment triggered what I now call my existential crisis.

For days, I kept replaying the interview in my mind. Why couldn't I answer that question? Then, it hit me. I didn't have a good failure story to share because my entire life, I'd avoided failure at all costs. I had always played it safe.

But had playing it safe really helped me?

Was I truly living a life of my own choosing?

Was I happy? Was I fulfilled?

The answer to every single question was a big, fat 'no'.

That is when I knew that unless I took the time to figure out how I could live a life of greater meaning and purpose, I would always regret it. So I made a bold decision – I left behind my comfortable life in New York and moved to India in search of my truth.

I remember feeling terrified.

One day, I confided in a close friend about how moving to India felt like jumping off a cliff. I had no clear plan, just a calling to do something different. That's when he said something so profound, it forever changed my life.

'Yes, Bhavna, you are jumping off a cliff, but you know what? The universe will be there with open arms to catch you as you fall, because *the universe always rewards courage.*'

I still get goosebumps to this day when I recall that moment. He was right. Ever since that day, I have consciously sought to make every choice, every decision, every action of mine from a place of courage.

And do you know what that has brought me?

A life fully aligned with my values.

A career that allows me to positively impact the lives of countless women and men every single day.

And most importantly, a deep sense of contentment from knowing I am on the right path.

None of this would have happened if I hadn't chosen courage as a guiding value in my life.

My question to you: Tell me about a time when you failed. What did you learn from that experience?

Live a life of courage

2

Inside-Out or Outside-In?

On seeing beauty through the right lens

Growing up, I didn't feel pretty. Far from it.

When I was seven years old, in typical comedic fashion, I ran straight into the glass doors separating our living room and balcony, breaking my front milk teeth in the process. Despite repeated warnings not to touch them as they were coming in, I couldn't resist. Sure enough, my front teeth grew out crooked and protruded.

From that point on, I became 'the girl with the buck teeth'.

As I entered my teens, I grew increasingly self-conscious about my smile. I hated taking pictures and would often stare at my reflection in the mirror, only to end up in tears. Eventually, I decided enough was enough. Instead of wallowing in self-pity, I got braces to straighten my teeth.

Fast forward to age twenty-one. My mom, believing it would boost my confidence, encouraged me to enter a beauty pageant. So I did. And to my surprise, I won. In 2001, I was crowned Miss India New York.

For the next few years, my life was steeped in glamour

– speaking engagements, modelling gigs, fashion shows, acting, hosting TV shows, emceeing charity galas, you name it. I had all the external validation my younger self had craved.

But was I happier?

Not really.

Despite the dazzling lights and applause, I felt like I was trapped in an endless game of musical chairs, anxious that, at any moment, the music would stop and I'd be the only one left standing, wondering if I truly belonged.

I couldn't quite understand this lingering insecurity, not until I made a life-changing decision. I left behind my cushy life in New York in search of something deeper – my true purpose. Moving to India, I immersed myself in a spiritual exploration of what it means to feel truly rooted in oneself.

What I discovered changed everything. As philosopher and psychologist William James has shared, each of us has two selves: the 'I' self – who sees and the 'me' self – who is seen.

Both are essential to your identity – observing the world *and* being mindful of how you are being observed, so you can adjust your behaviour and actions accordingly. You need a healthy balance between the two, but one is more essential for our well-being.

In *Build the Life You Want*, happiness researcher and Harvard professor Arthur Brooks emphasizes the importance of living from the inside-out – as a subject with agency to take action for the benefit of others – rather than the outside-in – as a passive object. Instead of constantly evaluating yourself based on how others see you, true happiness comes from asking: *How am I looking at the world? What am I doing for others?*

When you shift your perspective from *outside-in* to *inside-out*, your sense of self stabilizes. You become less dependent on external approval and more anchored in your own values and purpose.

This shift, which was further reinforced with my mindfulness practice, made a world of difference for me.

The more I consciously chose to live and lead from within, the more I began to see beauty – not just in myself but everywhere. I saw beauty in others, in my purpose, in the countless small and meaningful moments that make up this short but precious life.

Most importantly, I finally saw beauty in myself. Not the fleeting kind that is defined by comparison, but the deep-rooted kind that makes you feel secure, comfortable and utterly at peace in your own skin.

So how can you shift your focus? What would it mean for you to stop asking *'How do others see me?'* and instead ask, *'How am I looking at the world?'*

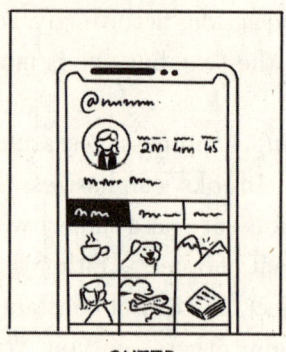

OUTER

INNER

3

Fear or Adventure?

On answering the call to adventure

Joseph Campbell, a renowned mythologist, set out to study the myths of legendary heroes from different cultures to answer one fundamental question – is there a pattern to a hero's journey?

The answer, to his delight, was a resounding *yes*.

He discovered that every hero, across time and space, passes through twelve distinct stages in their journey. These stages were so universal that they became a blueprint for storytelling, shaping everything from ancient epics to modern blockbusters. If you've watched *The Lion King* or the *Harry Potter* series, you've already witnessed Campbell's hero's journey in action.

The first stage is what Campbell calls the *'call to adventure'*. This is when the hero is invited to step beyond their ordinary world into the unknown, what Campbell refers to as the *'special world'*.

In *The Lion King*, Simba's call to adventure arrives when he sees the spirit of his father, Mufasa, who urges him to return to the Pride Lands and reclaim his rightful place as king.

In *Harry Potter and the Philosopher's Stone*, the call comes in the form of a letter from Hogwarts, summoning Harry to a world of magic and possibility.

At first glance, you'd think a hero upon receiving such an invitation would leap at the opportunity. You'd expect them to step forward with courage and enthusiasm, ready to embark on their journey.

But that's not what happens.

Here's the surprising truth: nearly every hero refuses the call at first.

Every hero, right after they receive or think of their call to adventure, has the instinct to say 'no'. This is the next step in nearly *every* hero's journey. Campbell calls this 'the refusal'.

Simba rejects his destiny. Overwhelmed by guilt, he runs away and tries to live a carefree life in exile, avoiding the responsibility he was born for. Harry struggles to believe that he is special. He hesitates, uncertain about leaving behind the only world he has ever known.

Why does this happen? Because, like you and me, heroes experience fear. They have the same doubts:

What if I fail?

What if people judge me?

What if I succeed, and my life changes in ways I'm not ready for?

This is where Campbell's insight is so powerful: A hero's fears hold the seed of their transformation. The very thing they are afraid of is the thing they must move toward.

Just like any hero, your fears are signposts. They signal that you are stepping outside your comfort zone into the

Fear or Adventure?

unknown. You don't yet know if you'll fail or succeed, but one thing is certain: *you will evolve.* You will grow into the person capable of meeting the challenges ahead.

Your fears are not barriers; they are invitations. They are pointing you toward the life, purpose and transformation that await.

So the question isn't *'Should I be afraid?'* It is *'Am I willing to say yes to this adventure knowing it will transform me?'*

As Robert Frost wrote, *'The best way out is always through.'*

My question to you: What adventure is calling to you right now? And will you say *yes*?

4

Possible or Impossible?
On the choice that changes everything

For years, it was widely accepted that no human being could run a mile in under four minutes. Scientists, coaches and even doctors insisted that it was physically impossible. They believed the human body wasn't designed to sustain such a pace; that if someone even attempted it, their heart might give out.

Then, on 6 May 1954, Roger Bannister shattered that belief. He ran a mile in 3 minutes and 59.4 seconds, proving that the four-minute barrier was not a physical limit, but a *mental* one.

What happened next was even more fascinating.

Just forty-six days later, John Landy, an Australian runner, broke the record again with a time of 3 minutes and 58 seconds. A year later, in a single race, three runners broke the four-minute barrier *together*. Over the decades since, more than a thousand runners have done what was once deemed impossible.

So what changed? Did humans suddenly evolve? Did a new breed of genetically superior runners emerge?

No. The only thing that changed was the *belief* of what was possible.

For years the idea of writing a book felt like an impossible dream for me.

I had a hundred excuses to justify why it wasn't the right time.

I'm too busy.

I'll do it later.

I need more experience.

Who am I to write a book?

I convinced myself that writing a book was something only *other* people did – seasoned authors, thought leaders, people with endless time and perfect discipline.

Then one day, someone gifted me a book written by another thought leader in my field. As I flipped through the pages, something clicked.

This person had a style of writing that felt so familiar. Their ideas, their approach, weren't *so* different from mine. And suddenly, a new thought entered my mind: *Wait a minute ... I can do this too.*

That tiny shift in thinking changed everything. Before long, I was excitedly sketching out an outline for my own book. The project that had felt impossible for years suddenly felt *within reach*.

And the only thing that changed? The voice in my head.

Bannister's story, my book-writing journey and countless other breakthroughs all point to the same truth: Whether something is possible or impossible is often a conscious choice, one that determines what we allow ourselves to pursue.

As Wharton School professors Yoram Wind and Colin Crook explain in *The Power of Impossible Thinking*, runners before Bannister were trapped by a mindset that told them the four-minute mile was unbreakable. But the moment Bannister proved it *could* be done, the belief system shifted. Suddenly it was no longer a question of *if* but *when*.

The same applies to every aspect of our lives. We tell ourselves, *I could never switch careers at this stage. I'm not smart enough to start my own business. Public speaking? I could never do that!*

But are these really *truths* or just mental barriers we've accepted?

Bannister's story reminds us that the biggest limits in life are often self-imposed.

Once you see someone else break through, it shifts your perspective. What was once impossible suddenly feels *within reach*. And that's where real transformation begins.

So what's your version of the four-minute mile?

What have you convinced yourself is impossible for you, simply because no one around you has done it yet?

Because here's the thing: impossible is just possible that hasn't been done yet.

My question to you: What's the impossible thing you are ready to make possible?

Possible or Impossible?

Go from

THIS to THIS

5

What or Why?

On asking the right questions

For many of us our father is our first hero – the one we look up to for strength, protection and guidance in building a remarkable life. That was certainly the case for me.

My father, a man of uncommon determination and principle, lifted himself and our family out of poverty through sheer hard work. He helped us all build lives in which we could dream of better opportunities for ourselves. After an illustrious career as an ambassador and diplomat with the Indian Foreign Service, he retired only to be diagnosed with Parkinson's shortly after.

He had many hopes and dreams for how he would live post-retirement, the ways he would continue serving his community. But as his strength waned, those dreams slipped away, leaving him with just one question: *why?*

Why did this happen to me? Why did this happen now? *Why?*

It's a question that comes up for many of us when we feel stuck in some way, when we want to change something about ourselves or our circumstances but just don't know how. At such times, in a desperate attempt to make sense of the situation, we often resort to asking, 'Why am I this way? Why do I keep doing this? Why does this keep happening?'

The problem is that asking *why* doesn't always help. As self-awareness researcher Tasha Eurich points out, *'why'* questions can keep us stuck in a cycle of negativity rather than providing real insight.

For example, let's say you yell at your child and then ask yourself, *'Why do I keep doing this?'* You might answer, *'Because I'm a bad mother.'* Even if the real reasons are that you were tired, stressed or hungry, *'why'* questions often lead to self-judgment rather than constructive solutions.

What's a better alternative? Replace your 'why' with a 'what'.

Instead of '*Why* do I always hesitate to speak up?' ask, '*What* can I do to speak up more?'

Instead of '*Why* do I keep falling back into old habits?' ask, '*What* can I do differently that will make this habit stick?'

Instead of '*Why* is my life or career stuck?' ask, '*What* is one small step I can take to improve my life or career?'

Eurich's research shows that people who ask themselves more 'what' questions experience higher levels of both self-awareness and self-improvement. Where a 'why' question might keep you stuck, a 'what' question has the power to open your mind to new solutions and insights, which can then help you accept your present circumstances and move forward.

It's been heartbreaking to see my father struggle with Parkinson's, but I am determined to do everything I can to ensure he still has a high quality of life. Instead of asking, 'Why did this happen?', I started asking, 'What can I do now?' The more I asked, the more helpful ideas I was able to find and put into action – from small things like helping him get back to his love of singing with online music classes to helping him document his life story with the help of a ghostwriter.

My question to you: What is something you would like to change? How can you move forward by asking yourself a powerful 'what' question?

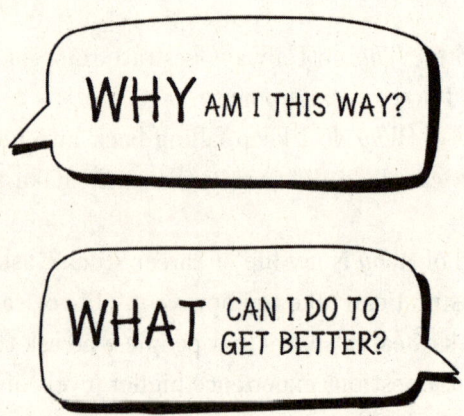

6

Character or Skill?
On finding hidden potential

Throughout our lives, whether in school or the workplace, we are taught that the more skilled you are, the more successful you will be. But what about your character? How much do traits such as honesty and integrity matter?

Fortunately, I have a research-backed answer for you.

A team of researchers ran a study with 1,500 entrepreneurs in Africa. With one group of entrepreneurs, the focus was on helping them develop cognitive skills such as finance, accounting and marketing. The other group focused on building character traits such as being proactive and disciplined in pursuing opportunities.

The result? The second group – the one focused on building character traits – grew their profits by 30% over two years. This was nearly three times the benefit of training in cognitive skills.

All this to say, as Adam Grant writes in *Hidden Potential*, if you want to unlock uncommon success for yourself, don't just look to improve your cognitive skills. In an AI-driven world where most cognitive skills will inevitably become automated, the skills that make you uniquely human – your character – will give you an edge.

Great. But how exactly can you build your character? The answer lies in both ancient philosophical traditions and modern science.

A core idea that ancient Chinese thinkers such as Confucius and Lao-Tzu expressed in their work was helping people experience a state of *wu-wei* (pronounced oo-way), which can be loosely translated as noble or virtuous action. To effortlessly engage in correct action, one must routinely cultivate what is known as *de* (pronounced duh) or 'virtue'. A virtue is a core characteristic or quality that is considered morally good and contributes to a fulfilling and meaningful life.

Martin Seligman, the father of positive psychology, explored whether a similar idea could be found among other major ancient belief systems – be it Christianity, Buddhism or Hinduism – and the answer was a resounding YES. If there is one thing all of these traditions share, it is living with virtue.

Seligman and his colleagues identified six core virtues that are present across cultures and throughout history. These are Wisdom, Courage, Humanity, Justice, Temperance and Transcendence.

Each of these six virtues further branch out into twenty-four sub-virtues or what they call Character Strengths. For example, Humanity further breaks down into Love, Kindness and Social Intelligence. Their research shows that individuals who are aware of their character strengths are nine times more likely to flourish.

Flourishing, according to Seligman, is finding fulfilment, accomplishing meaningful and worthwhile goals and connecting with others at a deeper level – in essence, living the 'good life'.

As both ancient philosophy and modern science demonstrate, if you want to build the strongest foundation for a life of greater happiness, meaning and even success, strengthening your character is the best place to start.

So my question to you is: What character strengths are you most focused on building?

7

Open Doors or Close Them?
On managing choices

A while ago, my husband and I went shopping for a coffee machine. We wanted a simple replacement for our previous one that had broken down, but we ended up buying a bigger, fancier model than we needed.

Why? Because we thought, 'Look! This one has a milk frother. Think of all the cappuccinos we could make and serve!' How many times have we actually used the milk frother since we got the machine? Zero.

We fall into this trap in many areas of our lives. We are wired to go for more options – to keep as many doors open as possible – with the mindset that you never know when you might need that option.

And so, we buy gadgets with more features than we need. We hold on to clothes for years, long after they've gone out of fashion or no longer fit. We fill our children's schedules with multiple activities, despite the toll it might take on them because we want to give them as many opportunities as possible. In our careers, too we keep pondering all the different paths we could take.

Open Doors or Close Them?

But as Dan Ariely writes in *Predictably Irrational*, for every door that you keep open, you pay a price – not just monetarily (the more the options the higher the price) but also psychologically. In trying to be everything you could be, do everything you could do or have all that you could have, you may forget where to draw the line.

Looking at my own life, every door that I have closed has only made me happier. I've been on a multi-year shopping fast and choosing not to buy new clothes has brought me so much peace of mind. I've made a firm commitment to avoid social media for the first few hours of my day, which frees up mental space to focus on what truly matters. In my work, I have chosen not to take on certain types of consulting projects or to work with certain kinds of clients. This clarity and focus has allowed me to grow my business exponentially over the last decade.

We may think having more options is better, but research shows closing certain doors might be the key to greater happiness and peace of mind. Fewer options create a greater sense of commitment to your chosen path, reduce decision fatigue and help you focus on what matters most. As Barry Schwartz writes in the *Paradox of Choice*, 'Choose less and feel better.'

So the question I would like to leave you with is: What are some doors you could consciously choose to close?

22   The Conscious Choice

8

Focus on Actions or Outcomes?
On mindful goal-setting

The Stoics had a wonderful expression called Deo volente. It loosely translates to 'God willing' or 'If fate will have it'. It was a qualifier added when expressing one's wishes or goals.

'I will travel around the world, *if fate will have it.*'

'I will lead an army, *if fate will have it.*'

It sounds like a passive expression, as if you are simply transferring all responsibility for your success to fate. In reality, this phrase is about remembering what is and isn't within your control.

Sure, it's important to set lofty goals that give you a sense of direction. But once you have set the goal, you must forget it. Instead, turn your attention to what is within your control – the steps you can take to reach that goal.

And the end result? Well, that you leave to fate.

We find the same idea in the *Bhagavad Gita*, an ancient Hindu scripture that describes Karma yoga as one of the four paths to spiritual liberation. Karma yoga or the 'path of action', urges you to perform your actions without attachment to a particular result. Once again, it's a reminder to do your best, to do the right thing, though the outcome may be out of your hands.

Often, in our pursuit of success, we become so goal-obsessed that the predominant question in our minds becomes 'Am I there yet? Am I there yet? Am I there yet?'

We constantly look at the gap between where we are and where we would like to be and if the gap is not to our liking, we feel incomplete or unworthy.

In what I like to call mindful goal setting, once you pick a worthy goal, the next step is to break it down into a set of actions you must undertake to reach it. You then shine the spotlight of the mind entirely on the tasks at hand. That way your feelings of success and happiness rest not on how far away you are from reaching your goal, but on asking:

'Did I show up fully today and approach my task as best as I could?'

If you did, then every day you get to experience completeness – to rejoice, rather than leaving celebration to some distant point in the future.

And for everything else, you can say, 'Deo volente – if fate will have it.'

My questions for you: What is a goal that is meaningful to you? How can you focus less on the outcome and more on the actions you take today?

Focus on Actions or Outcomes?

9

Feedback or Feed-forward?
On future-focused improvement

Feedback can truly be a gift. The problem is our need for feedback sits at the intersection of two core but competing human needs.

On one hand, you have a genuine desire to learn and grow and you seek information that helps you do exactly that. On the other hand, you also crave a sense of belonging, and to be loved and accepted exactly as you are.

That is why receiving feedback can make us feel vulnerable and even defensive – if what we hear is less ideal, our very sense of self can feel threatened. It can evoke painful feelings of inadequacy ('Am I good enough?') or embarrassment ('Does this make me look bad?').

Neuroimaging studies have shown that the brain processes social pain the same way as it does physical pain. If I slip and fall, and you laugh at me, my embarrassment may be just as painful as the physical impact of the injury. Given that we are naturally wired to protect ourselves from any pain, the possibility of social pain that comes with feedback is why we instinctively resist it.

Feedback or Feed-forward?

Negative feedback can be particularly damaging if you strongly identify with your work. As researchers Rafeli and Gleason note, 'If you have a belief that you are your work, it [feedback] can erode the core of your self-confidence.'

So how can we help each other become better without the fear that feedback can create?

We can make a simple but profound change by shifting the lens through which we approach self-improvement. Move from feedback – which is focused on the unchangeable past – to what renowned leadership coach Marshall Goldsmith calls feed-forward, aimed at creating a better future.

For example, let's say being seen as someone who is a good listener is important to you. Instead of asking for feedback on whether you are a good listener, you might ask for feed-forward on how you can *become* a better listener. Or say you want to improve your communication skills. Instead of asking for feedback on your last presentation, you could ask for feed-forward on how you can become a better presenter, going forward.

The biggest benefit of this forward-looking approach is that it takes judgment out of the conversation, creating a safe space for more open and honest communication. When the person giving you feedback feels like their input can help you create a better future, they are more open in sharing their ideas. And without the threat of judgment, you as the receiver are more likely to receive the feedback with grace and take action.

The renowned mindfulness teacher Thich Nhat Hanh once said that the most precious words you can offer a loved one are:

'How can I love you better?'

Such a powerful example of seeking feed-forward, aimed at creating a more loving future together.

Similarly, another feed-forward question I'd like to leave you with – and encourage you to ask anyone you care about in your life, whether in a personal or professional capacity – is:

'How can I support you better?'

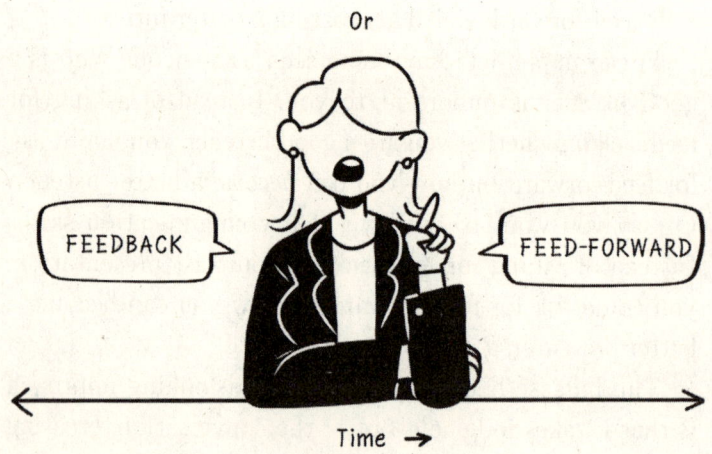

10

Static Opinions or Working Hypotheses?

On embracing intellectual flexibility

Here's a question for you: How do you react when someone challenges an opinion that you hold?

Do you listen calmly, or do you get defensive?

We'd like to believe we are rational creatures, able to easily change our minds when presented with a new set of facts. The truth is, it can be a deeply uncomfortable experience because our opinions become closely tied to our identity.

For instance, if you believe in climate change, your identity becomes that of an environmentalist. If you don't believe in the efficacy of vaccines, you are labeled an anti-vaxxer. If you believe in equality for all genders, you are a feminist.

Now, I consider myself a feminist. If you question my opinions on issues related to gender equality, I may feel you are not just challenging my opinions, but questioning my worldview – even my very identity as a feminist. That feels threatening – it can feel like an existential crisis.

But if we hold our opinions too closely, how do we make room for new growth and learning? How do we make progress?

Here's a thought-provoking suggestion from Ozan Varol that can help us become less attached to our opinions – think like a scientist! When you think like a scientist, you don't form a fixed opinion – you form what is called a working hypothesis.

A working hypothesis, by definition, is a work in progress. It is open to being tested and adapted in the face of new information.

Try applying this to the opinions you hold.

Instead of saying, 'I believe technology X is the answer to all our problems,' you might say, 'I have a working hypothesis that technology X can solve a lot of problems.'

Instead of saying, 'I believe this is the best move to make for my career,' you might say, 'I have a working hypothesis that this move could benefit my career.'

This simple shift in language can trick your mind into being more curious, flexible and open to being wrong. Will this work in all situations? Maybe not. But what a wonderful world it will be if we all allow ourselves a little more room to change our perspective – to look at the world with fresh eyes.

So the question I leave you with is: What opinion of yours are you willing to turn into a working hypothesis?

Static Opinions or Working Hypotheses?

11

Schadenfreude or Freudenfreude?

On finding joy in others' success

Back in school, in sixth grade, I was in the running to become the Head Girl. It was a highly coveted role as a student leader, and to be honest, I thought my chances of getting it were slim since I wasn't always a star student.

All I remember is my dear friend Sonia was my biggest supporter at the time. When, to my utter surprise, it was announced that I was going to be the next Head Girl of the school, her excitement went through the roof.

I can picture the moment like it was yesterday – Sonia jumping up and down, furiously clapping her hands and grinning from ear-to-ear. She spent the rest of the day bouncing around as if she had won the title.

What Sonia demonstrated that day was freudenfreude – for me, a beautiful lesson for life.

You may have heard of the expression schadenfreude – the pleasure one feels when witnessing someone's misfortune. For example, feeling happy when a rival sports team loses. Freudenfreude on the other hand, is finding joy in another person's good fortune. Inspired by the German word for joy, it describes the bliss we feel when someone else succeeds, even if it doesn't directly involve us.

It's natural to experience a twinge of jealousy or even sadness when you witness someone else's success. For those of us conditioned to treat success as a zero-sum game – 'Your win is my loss' – because of childhood experiences of being pitted against others and only having your achievements rewarded, it's easy for our self-worth to take a hit when someone else succeeds.

When you consciously practise freudenfreude, you avoid the downward spiral of shame and self-loathing that can come from comparing yourself to others and instead experience a whole host of benefits. A 2021 study by researcher Gregory John Depow and others found practising positive empathy – essentially, freudenfreude – enhances our tendency to perform kind acts. Additionally, participating in the happiness of others was found to boost resilience, life satisfaction and cooperation in times of conflict.

While freudenfreude may not be a feeling that comes naturally to us, we can train ourselves to express it with sincerity. To help individuals build their capacity for sharing joy, Dr Catherine Chambliss and her team created a programme known as Freudenfreude Enhancement Training (FET). Below are two exercises from the programme that you can adopt:

One, practise 'shoy' – actively share in the joy of others. One way to do this is by asking more questions about their big win. 'Tell me more!' 'How do you feel right now?' 'How are you planning to celebrate?'

Two, practise 'bragitude' – express gratitude to the person sharing their good news. You might say, 'Thank you for sharing that with me' or 'Thanks for inspiring me'.

As Sonja Lyubomirsky's research shows, when you share in the joy of others, your own happiness multiples and your relationships deepen. The next time someone shares their joy with you, embody my childhood friend Sonia and say, 'Wow, congratulations! Tell me all about it. And then, let's go out and celebrate!'

My question to you: How can you practise more freudenfreude this year?

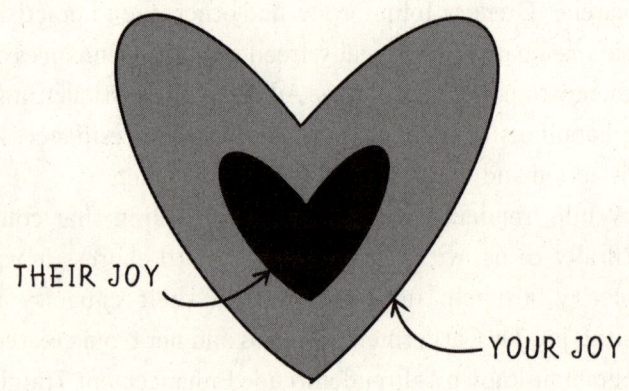

12

Self-Judgment or Self-Awareness?

On turning comparison into growth

Do you ever experience a twinge of envy when you come across someone on social media who's doing really well professionally, or looks great, or is off on some exotic vacation?

Do you find these feelings soon morphing into some form of self-criticism or even shame? You hear thoughts like, 'Gosh, what am I doing with my life. I should be doing more. I am not successful enough, or fit enough, or good enough.'

If the answer is yes, know that strong evolutionary forces programme your mind to think this way. Back in the Stone Age, it was essential to our survival to be in a constant state of comparison – wondering, 'Am I fitting into my group?' or 'Am I as valuable to the group as everyone else?' After all, losing the acceptance or protection of your tribe could have meant the difference between life and death.

It doesn't help that now in the age of social media that small tribe has expanded to over eight billion people. Fortunately, we can protect ourselves from falling into this constant comparison mode. Here's a different approach that works for me.

Whenever you are triggered by comparison and find yourself going down a rabbit hole of self-criticism and shame, try to convert that moment of judgment into a moment of self-awareness by asking yourself:

What is this telling me about what's important to me?

Oftentimes, this will reveal to you an area of your life that you might be neglecting. If you are triggered by someone's six-pack abs, it could be because you wish you were healthier. If you are triggered by someone sharing their ideas on LinkedIn, maybe it's because you secretly wish you had the courage to share your ideas more publicly.

Armed with that self-awareness, you gain clarity and can then choose to take action towards the things that truly matter to you – whether that's advancing your career, improving your fitness or creating more space for adventure in your life.

A core principle of mindfulness is that judgment and curiosity cannot coexist. So the next time you find yourself slipping into judgment, I invite you to shift to a space of curiosity instead. Use your triggers as a learning opportunity to understand who you are and what you value.

Ask these two questions next time. First: What is triggering self-judgment in me? Next: What could my self-judgment be telling me about what is important to me?

Self-Judgment or Self-Awareness?

WHAT IT FEELS LIKE

WHAT IT ACTUALLY IS

13

I Don't or I Can't?
On empowered refusals

Is there a habit you've been trying to change for a while, but are finding it difficult to do so? Maybe you want to eat better or exercise more so you can be fitter, but you struggle to resist those late-night cravings.

Or maybe, like me, you want more time for what is most important to you, such as focusing on your personal development or an important side project. But at the end of a long, hard day, you find it easier to lose precious hours on Netflix or social media.

How do you change a habit that has a strong hold on you? As it turns out, the way you frame your choice has a lot to do with it.

Imagine this: Preeti and Ruchi both want to change their diet and have similar weight loss goals. Every time they see a chocolate cake, Preeti says 'Oh, I *can't* eat chocolate cake.' On the other hand, Ruchi says, 'I *don't* eat chocolate cake.' Who do you think is going to be more successful in sticking to a healthy diet in the long run?

According to research by Professor Vanessa Patrick,

saying 'I don't' is eight times more effective than saying 'I can't'.

When you say 'I can't', it implies that you have to exert a lot of control to go against your wishes, which can be exhausting. On the other hand, saying 'I don't' implies you are making a conscious choice. Patrick calls this an empowered refusal – a firm and decisive stance that does not invite pushback, either from yourself or others. You are saying: This is what I do and this is what I don't do. You are giving voice to your values, priorities and preferences.

The key thing to consider is how the words you use shape your identity. Saying 'I can't' binds you to the old identity that you are trying so hard to change. Whereas saying 'I don't' helps you adopt a new identity that is more supportive of the habits you are trying to form.

The question I leave you with is: What is something that you *don't* do?

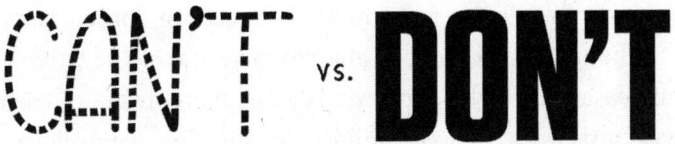

14

Step In or Step Back?
On managing one's thoughts

Research shows we have an average of 60,000 to 70,000 thoughts a day. Do you know how many of these typically lean toward the negative? Up to 80%!

This is all thanks to the amygdala, which sits in the oldest part of the brain and is constantly scanning our environment for threats or problems. While this is a useful function when it comes to our survival, it doesn't help our mental well-being to constantly look out for what is wrong or could go wrong. A negatively-biased brain can make it quite challenging to feel any kind of peace or contentment.

Though you may not be able to entirely avoid negative or unpleasant thoughts, you *can* become more aware of them with practices such as mindful meditation. Consciously train yourself to create some space and distance from these thoughts by using seven powerful words: 'I notice I am having the thought ...'

For example:

While getting ready for an important conversation you think, 'This might not go well.' Instead, pause and tell yourself, 'I notice I am having the thought that this might not go well.'

It's one of those days where you feel nothing is going your way and you think, 'This is a terrible day.' Pause and tell yourself, 'I notice I am having the thought that this day is terrible.'

A recent project didn't quite deliver the results you were hoping for, and you are now thinking, 'Gosh, I feel like a complete failure.' Pause and rethink: 'I notice I am having the thought that I feel like a failure.'

At every juncture, you have two choices – to step into the thought or to step back from it. Creating space between yourself and your thoughts opens your mind to new choices, different possibilities and healthier ways of processing them.

Sometimes, simply shining the spotlight of your awareness on the thought makes it weaker, allowing you to see it as just another fleeting moment in the mind's endless chatter. You can then mindfully replace the thought with a better feeling one. For instance, 'I notice I am having the thought that this might not go well. Let me think of reasons why it will go well.'

As Holocaust survivor Viktor Frankl wrote in *Man's Search for Meaning*:

> Between stimulus and response, there is a space. In that space lies our power to choose our response. In our response, lies our growth and our freedom.

When you step back to notice your thoughts, you create

space to think and act differently, and gain freedom from thoughts that don't serve you well.

So what are you becoming present to in this moment? Complete this sentence: 'I notice I am having the thought ...'

15

Purpose or Passion?
On finding meaning in work

When we look at the most successful people around us, it appears they are driven by a deep sense of both passion and purpose. But is one of these motivators more important than the other for success?

Let's break it down.

Your work feels purposeful when it has broader meaning and allows you to contribute to the lives of others. Passion, on the other hand, is the feeling of excitement or enthusiasm you experience about your work.

Which one do you think leads to greater job performance?

Professor Morten Hansen, who teaches Management at the University of California, Berkeley, studied more than 5,000 managers and employees to discover how they maximize their time and performance.

His findings revealed that the top performers were people who had both passion and purpose – no surprise there. Similarly, as you would expect, people who lacked both passion and purpose were ranked among the worst performers. But what about those in the middle – the majority?

It turns out that people who had a certain amount of excitement or passion for their work were still considered poor performers ... *if they lacked purpose.* In other words, purpose trumps passion.

Here's why: Passion is all about you. It's about what excites you. It can be individualistic and even isolating because your passion may not be the same as mine. Purpose on the other hand is something we can share. In fact, research shows that the highest-performing teams are effective *because* they unite around a common purpose. When team members share a clear and meaningful goal, it enhances motivation and aligns individual efforts toward a collective vision, ultimately driving higher performance and success.

So how can you cultivate purpose in your work? By asking yourself this one crucial question: *How does my work benefit others?*

The good news is, even if you're not particularly passionate about what you are doing right now, as long as you are clear about how your work helps others, you will ignite a sense of purpose that energizes you to perform well.

This is especially relevant for managers. Knowing that clarity on the team's purpose is crucial, you can take extra care to connect the dots for every single person on your team. Help each individual see how their work contributes to the team's larger goals and you will cultivate a shared sense of purpose.

While the winning combination is to have both passion and purpose, if you have to choose, prioritize purpose over passion.

The question I leave you with is: What about your work do you find purposeful?

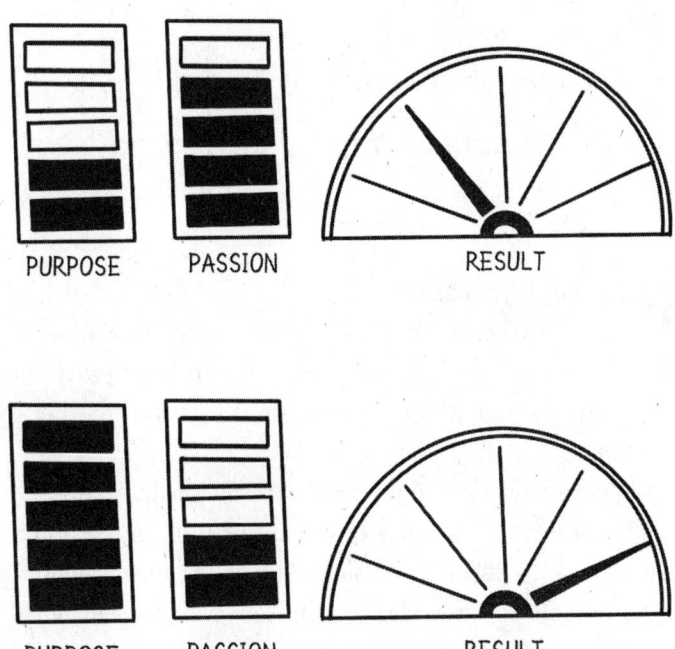

16

Addition or Subtraction?
On simplifying by letting go

Imagine this scenario:
I ask you to build a simple bridge using Lego blocks. I give you a model of an existing bridge to begin with, but it is uneven – one of its pillars is shorter than the other by one block.

What would you do next to make the bridge even?

If you are like most people, you would simply add an extra block to the shorter side. This is because a majority of us default to an *addition* mindset. When faced with a challenge, our default instinct is to think about what we can add to make something better.

If I asked you to improve a travel itinerary, you would think of what activities you could add to it. If I asked you to improve a recipe, you would think of all the additional ingredients that might enhance it.

Now, think of the kind of changes you aim to bring about in your life and career this year. Chances are, your instinct is to want *more* – more opportunities, more achievements, more success, more money. The word growth itself indicates increase.

While addition has its value, it can quickly become overwhelming – chasing multiple goals, juggling a never-ending to-do list or living in a home cluttered with stuff. What if you could make something better by subtracting instead? By asking: What can I say no to? What can I let go of?

As Leidy Klotz reminds us in *Subtract*, 'A poet knows he has achieved perfection not when there is nothing left to add, but when there is nothing left to take away.' Subtraction can be an overlooked force for positive change in our lives. As you move forward with your journey of growth, I encourage you to also look at what you wish to let go of.

For instance, I know the more I let go of my need for control, the more room I will create for spontaneity and creativity. The more I let go of appearing perfect, the more authentic my connections become. The more I let go of the fear of judgment, the more risks I can take with my work.

As Lao Tzu said, 'To attain knowledge, add things every day. To attain wisdom, remove things every day.'

Coming back to the Lego bridge, removing a block from the longer pillar is just as effective as adding one to the shorter pillar. And so it is with life – sometimes, growth comes from not adding but from letting go. Learning how to subtract mindfully can help ease our mental burdens, reduce anxiety and give us more freedom to focus on what truly matters.

The question I leave you with is: What ideas or things would you like to subtract from your life?

48   The Conscious Choice

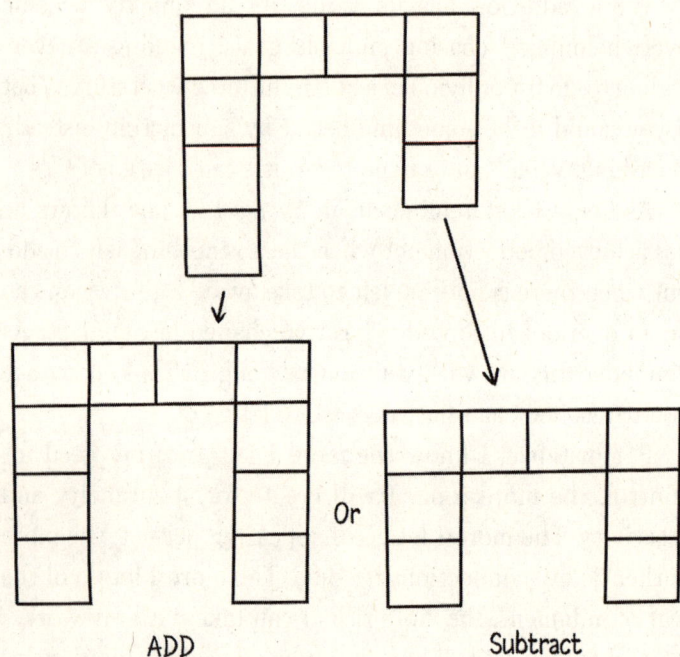

ADD   Or   Subtract

17

Raise the Bar or Lower It?

On balancing ambition with achievable goals

One thing I find with a lot of ambitious, high achievers is that we are almost always experiencing some level of discontent with ourselves.

Does this sound like you? You set the bar extremely high – you want your work to be of the highest quality, you want to be a supermom, you want to be super-fit, you want a vibrant social life ... the list is endless. Worst of all, you constantly compare where you are with where you would like to be, using that as a measure of how good you are allowed to feel about yourself.

A lot of this is not your fault. The culture we live in conditions us to always strive for more – to think big, to set audacious goals and want it all. But what that also means is that it can become incredibly easy to feel like a failure, a lot of the time.

Here's a paradox I've discovered: the more I lower my standards for success, the more successful I become.

Let me share a small example:

A couple of years ago, I decided to take charge of my physical fitness. Fed up with feeling bloated and lethargic, I decided to push myself into high gear by entering a twelve-week fitness challenge. After being minimally active through the pandemic, I thought this would be a fun way to get back in shape.

This was not my first attempt to transform my physical fitness, but it *was* the most successful. What made the difference?

In the past I struggled with thoughts like, 'Oh, I don't have sixty minutes to work out' or 'I can't work out three or four times a week.' I had an all-or-nothing attitude.

This time, I told myself that as long as I worked out for fifteen minutes a day – not forty-five, not thirty, just fifteen minutes – I would consider that a success. I downloaded a fitness app that provided short, at-home workouts and found myself exercising more frequently because, 'Hey, it's only fifteen minutes!' Over time, I built endurance and started working out for longer periods.

To my surprise, this approach worked beautifully. So well that at the end of the twelve weeks, I ranked in the top fifty among more than 40,000 participants in the challenge.

The surprising benefit of lowering the bar is that it allows you to climb over it more easily. This helps you take the first step, achieve small wins and build the momentum to keep going.

As James Clear shares in his bestselling book *Atomic Habits*, this is a fundamental law of behavioural change. When you focus on lowering the bar and making a habit easy to start, you build consistency – and consistency, over time, compounds to produce astounding results.

Three years later, I am still going strong with my fitness routine. What's the secret behind my consistency? Even on my worst days, when working out is the last thing on my mind, I tell myself, 'How about I just go to the gym for fifteen minutes!'

The question I leave you with is: In what area of your life could you benefit from lowering your standards for success?

Time →

18

Pull Out the Thorn or Live Around It?

On navigating rejection

Like many Indian girls, I didn't grow up playing a lot of sports. It just wasn't encouraged in my time. As fate would have it, right around middle school, my family moved to London, and I enrolled in an all-girls school that happened to be big on sports.

I didn't have a single athletic bone in my body, or so I thought. I felt shy and self-conscious even wearing shorts during P.E. class and my awkwardness was palpable. Sure enough, I became that girl who was always picked last whenever teams were formed.

Rejection is painful – visceral even. Research shows that the brain equates social pain with physical pain. In other words, rejection literally feels like a punch in the gut.

Soon, the fear of rejection became so deeply ingrained in me, I began designing my whole life to protect myself from it.

It's like the analogy Michael Singer shares in his book, *The Untethered Soul*. If you get pricked by a thorn on your

Pull Out the Thorn or Live Around It?

foot and it stays lodged there, you have two options. One, you can design your whole life to shield your foot from anything that might – even accidentally – touch that thorn and ignite sharp pain. You can wear shoes with extra padding to cover your foot, avoid places where you might step the wrong way, even make sure no one comes too close to you. Two, you can be brave and simply pull the thorn out.

For years, I chose option one.

I only ever pursued things where there was a high probability of success. If there was even a remote possibility of hearing no, I wouldn't ask. I bent over backwards trying to be perfect, believing it would shield me from rejection.

With time, I realized that was a painful way to live. When I finally learned to live more consciously, I decided it was time to pick option two – to pull out the damned thorn. I knew that if I continued to live my life afraid of rejection by others, I would really be rejecting myself – the life that could be mine, the endless possibilities for my growth and evolution.

And so I began what I like to call The Great Rejection Experiment.

I started treating asking for all kinds of things like an experiment. If people said yes, great. If they said no, rather than take it personally, I simply asked myself three questions:

1. What did I do well here?
2. What can I learn from this?
3. How can I do better next time?

Over the years, I've asked for everything – from discounts on courses (I'm eternally grateful to those who mentored me when I couldn't afford their full-priced coaching) to raises (I doubled my income early on in my career simply because I asked and was able to justify the increase).

And perhaps most profoundly – for love.

I made the first move with my husband of over ten years. I saw him for the first time at a party and my intuition told me he was someone I would like to get to know. Unfortunately, we never managed to speak that day, but I wasn't ready to accept defeat and spend my life wondering 'What if ...'

So the next day, I reached out to him on Facebook. Long story short, a week after I sent that message, we met for our first date. A year later, we got engaged.

By gamifying asking for things, I took the sting out of rejection. At the same time, because I was always reflecting on what I could learn and improve, The Great Rejection Experiment became one of the most powerful levers of personal growth in my life.

As Nelson Mandela once said, 'I never lose. I either win or I learn.' And since learning is also a win, I now see it as: 'I win or I win'.

I've now experienced wins such as founding Shenomics and enlisting one Fortune 500 organization after another as a client. At the same time, losing a couple of big clients early on taught me where I could improve. This made way for other wins such as getting guidance from celebrity mentors on how I could make a bigger impact in the world. Wins such as building my visibility on LinkedIn, bracing rejection with each post and eventually becoming a LinkedIn Top Voice.

So let me ask you: What possibilities await you if you could simply pull out that thorn?

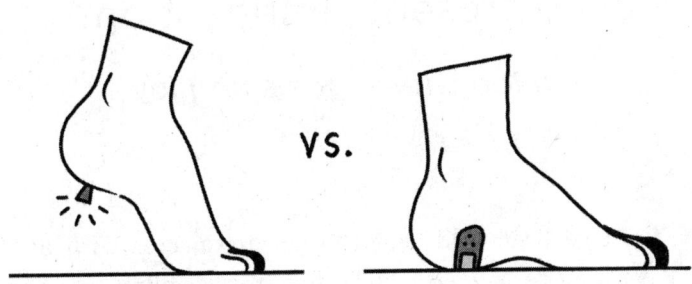

19

Delayed Gratification or Ever-present Gratification?

On long-term goals and joy

We've been told that the key to success with any long-term goal – whether it's excelling in your career, improving your financial well-being or getting fit – is delayed gratification. Make whatever sacrifices are needed today, so that one day, in the future, you can reap the rewards of your hard work.

Save money now so you can buy a house later. Put in the repetitions today so you can be fitter tomorrow. Work hard now for the promotion you want down the line. In fact, if you look at most ancient religions, the idea of making ritualistic offerings to a higher power stems from the same thinking. Give something today to gain something – blessings, good fortune or whatever it is that you desire – in the future.

On one hand, there is value in this. The benefits of hard work do compound over time. But there is also a cost to only living for a better tomorrow.

That better tomorrow may never come – or if it does, you might realize that buying the house, making more money or achieving a certain goal doesn't bring the happiness you expected. What then? Well, if you're like most people, you quickly move on to the next goal. Then the next. And the next. You keep postponing your happiness, seeing your constant discontent as a badge of honour – the price of success.

Could there be a better way than staying on this hamster wheel of striving and never arriving?

Dr Ellen Langer of Harvard University offers a powerful alternative. She calls it 'Ever-present Gratification' – the idea that instead of waiting for some distant future to feel fulfilled, you make the *process* of achieving your goals just as enjoyable and desirable as the final destination.

How can you do that?

By building joy and play into your daily routine. By allowing yourself a small treat every now and then, instead of being super strict with your diet. By making time for meaningful conversations with loved ones now, rather than waiting until you 'have more time'. By celebrating the many small milestones along the way, instead of only recognizing progress at the very end.

Not only does this make the journey of success far more fulfilling, but as Dr Andrew Huberman points out, it also helps rewire your brain's reward system. Instead of only getting a dopamine hit when you cross the finish line, you train your brain to release dopamine – the brain's reward hormone – at each step. This is what helps you build the grit and resilience needed to stay committed for the long haul.

From an evolutionary standpoint, the human brain is wired for immediate outcomes. If there was a raging storm, you would take shelter at once. If you stumbled upon a tree laden with fruit, you ate what you could, not knowing when you'd get another meal. If a tiger was chasing you, you didn't waste time thinking, you ran.

Given how strong our preference for immediate rewards is, instead of denying yourself joy, what if you *harnessed* this instinct? What if you made the daily pursuit of your long-term goals more rewarding?

Take another example: Dr. Michelle Segar, a leading behavioural science researcher, found that the most successful exercisers don't work out because of vague, long-term goals like *'I want to lose weight'* or *'I want to be healthier in the future.'* Instead, the people who exercise most consistently are those who give themselves a *concrete* and *immediate* why. For instance, *'I want to feel better in my body now.'*

In her study, only 25 per cent of participants focused on an *immediate* benefit, yet they exercised 30 per cent more than those focusing on long-term outcomes.

The takeaway? Don't let your happiness become a ritualistic sacrifice for some future destination. Instead, consciously choose joy in the here and now.

My question to you: How can you practise 'ever-present gratification' while working toward your long-term goals?

Delayed Gratification or Ever-present Gratification?

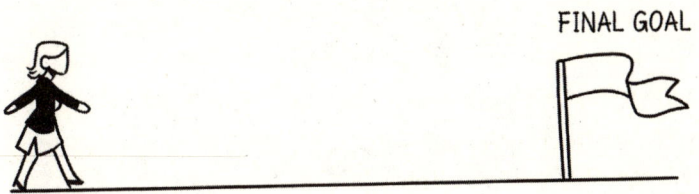

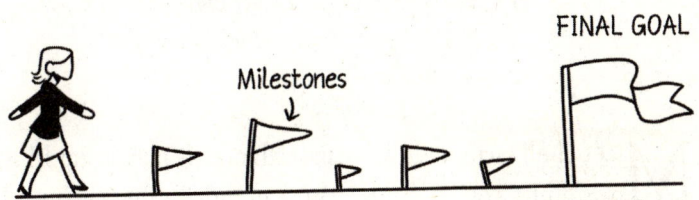

20

To Fall or To Rise Stronger?
On resilience and growth

Meet the Daruma doll. At first glance, it may seem like a simple, round figure. But behind its design lies a profound lesson of resilience – it is weighted at the bottom, allowing it to bounce back upright regardless of which direction it gets knocked in.

The Daruma doll is modelled after Bodhidharma, a renowned Buddhist monk. Just like the Buddha, Bodhidharma was a prince who left behind royalty to pursue a spiritual path. He is credited with spreading Buddhism across China and Japan in the fifth and sixth centuries. His meditation techniques became known as *Chan* in China and *Zen* in Japan.

To Fall or To Rise Stronger?

Legend has it Bodhidharma was so resolute in his determination to attain enlightenment that he meditated fiercely in a cave for nine years. His commitment was so unwavering that, over time, his arms and legs atrophied and fell off.

That is why Daruma dolls are never shown to have any limbs and are designed to be bottom-heavy – when knocked down, they bounce right back up. In fact, a popular reference for these dolls is '*Nana korobi ya oki*' – 'fall down seven, get up eight.'

The doll acts as a reminder to build an iron-willed resolve when pursuing a meaningful goal, one so deeply important that nothing can deter you from your chosen path.

The Daruma doll is also used as a goal-setting tool. When you set an intention, you fill in one eye of the doll. The blank eye serves as a visual reminder of your goal, encouraging you to stay committed. Once you achieve your goal, you fill in the second eye symbolizing completion and success.

I find this ritual deeply meaningful because it reminds us that progress isn't always linear. Setbacks are part of the journey. But as long as you keep going, you haven't failed.

What is a goal that is so noble and meaningful to you that you are willing to do whatever it takes to achieve it? A goal not driven by external measures of success like money or power – which research shows can bring only temporary happiness – but one anchored in internal fulfillment. Something that helps you learn, grow and evolve into a better version of yourself.

Maybe you want to be a kinder parent, no matter how often life – or even your child – tests you.

Maybe you want to immerse yourself in learning something, or mastering an old hobby, despite the inconvenience of making space for it in your life.

Maybe you want to do build something – a product, a business or an idea – that elevates the happiness and well-being of others, even in the face of obstacles.

And just like the Daruma doll, every time life knocks you down – disappointment, failure or adversity of any kind – you remind yourself: 'Fall down seven, get up eight.'

And then, you rise again.

So, my question to you is: Where in your life can you be more like a Daruma doll?

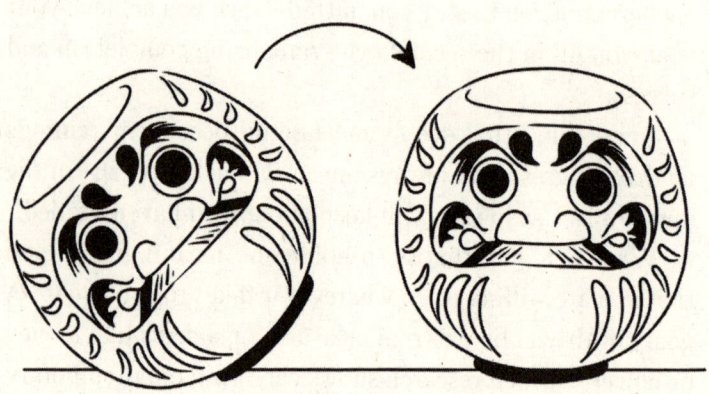

21

The First or the Second Arrow?
On responding to suffering

The Buddha once asked his student, 'If a person is struck by an arrow, is it painful?' The student nodded, 'Yes, it is.' He then asked, 'If a person is struck by a second arrow, is that even more painful?' Again, the student nodded, 'Yes, it would be.'

The Buddha explained, 'In life, we cannot always control the first arrow. However, the second arrow is our reaction to the first. The second arrow is optional.'

The first arrow is when someone makes an unkind remark. The second arrow is when you keep replaying that remark over and over again in your mind.

The first arrow is when you make a small mistake while giving a presentation. The second arrow is when you say, 'Gosh, how could I have been so stupid' and keep beating yourself up over it.

As Thich Nhat Hanh reminds us in *No Mud, No Lotus*, mud is essential to the creation and thriving of a beautiful lotus. Similarly, we can't build a flourishing, happy life without the presence or awareness of suffering. In fact, according to Buddhist tradition, suffering is the first of the four noble truths of our existence. Suffering is a given, and that is why Thich Nhat Hanh tells us if we are going to live well, then we must learn to 'suffer well'.

Repeatedly shooting ourselves with the second arrow is not how we suffer well. Quite the opposite – it causes us to lose our sense of balance and peace of mind.

So how can you stop yourself from shooting the second arrow? Try this simple but profound practice a mindfulness teacher taught me:

Ask, *what else is true?*

You made a mistake during a presentation. What else is true?

What else is true is that you worked really hard on that presentation. The majority of the presentation went just fine. In fact, many people appreciated what you shared.

You spoke harshly with your child and now feel guilty for being a 'bad parent'. What else is true?

What else is true is that you also shower your child with countless acts of love and affection every day. What else is true is that you are human and like any human being, have both good and bad days. What else is true is that you are committed to being a good parent. You have the capacity to reflect on your behavior and move forward in the most compassionate way possible for you and your child.

Asking this question allows you to see other truths in the situation that you may have missed. Seeing the full picture takes effort and intention, but if we consciously train ourselves to ask this question, we can bring the mind back to a state of stability, balance and centeredness.

So, next time you find your thoughts focusing only on the negative aspects of a situation, **I encourage you to simply widen your lens and ask:** What else is true?

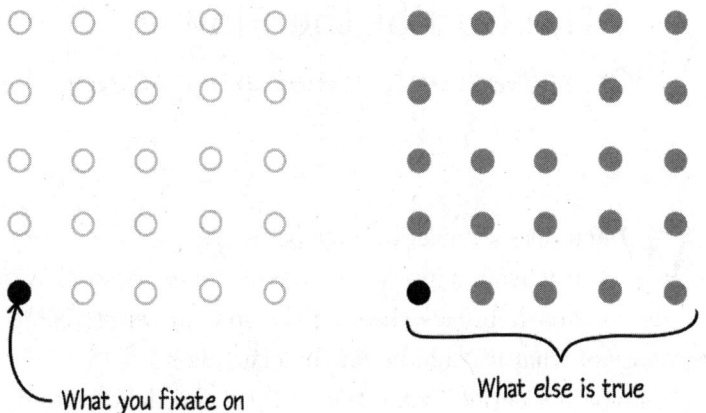

22

The Bud or the Flower?
On self-acceptance at every stage

When does a flower become perfect?

Is it when it's just a seed, full of endless possibility?

Is it when it breaks through the soil, showing visible promise of what it could be for the first time?

Maybe it's perfect when it's a gentle and delicate bud, on the verge of blossoming?

Could it be when it's in full bloom, showing the world all its magnificence? Or is it finally perfect when it reaches its humble end and returns to the same soil from which it came?

I think you already know the answer. The flower is perfect at every stage of its journey.

A flower is a specimen of nature, and everything in nature is exactly as it is intended to be. There are no imperfections. You, too, are a part of nature. That is something we often forget.

You go through life believing there is some end point of perfection you must reach before you can fully accept yourself – before you can finally be happy and at peace. I spent years on this proverbial 'achievement treadmill', my head filled with thoughts like:

'Once I am more successful, I will earn the right to be at peace with myself.'

'Once I shed all my "bad habits", I can finally feel proud of myself.'

'Once my level of fitness is where it "should be", only then can I give my body the love that it deserves.'

The strange thing is, no matter how hard I worked, I never arrived where I wanted to be. The destination – as elusive as it was to begin with – kept moving farther away. There was always another goal to chase. Perfection – waiting in the next moment ... or the moment after that. But never in the present.

It was only once I started practicing mindfulness that I realized I had it all backwards. My self-loathing was the very thing that was keeping me stuck and sabotaging my efforts at change. But when I started practising greater self-acceptance, I was finally able to ease my foot off the brakes and move forward.

As Carl Rogers said, 'The curious paradox is that when I accept myself just as I am, then I can change.'

The more I valued my own potential, the bigger the goals I set for myself. The kinder I was to myself, the more I pushed myself to achieve those goals – not for external validation but because of the immense faith I had in my own capabilities.

Pursuing my most cherished dreams felt like the greatest act of self-compassion. And the more I accepted failure as a normal part of my journey, instead of beating myself up over it, the more grace I gave myself to fall, get back up and try again.

We often believe we have to choose between growth and self-acceptance, that in order to grow we must be tough on ourselves – that if we practise self-compassion, we will become lazy or complacent. But the truth is, self-acceptance and growth can go hand in hand.

Every stage of a flower's journey is perfect – yet it never stops changing, growing and evolving. What if, like the flower, you see perfection in every phase of your journey? How might your experience of life change?

My question to you: How can you practise the self-acceptance and self-compassion you deserve in order to keep learning, growing and evolving?

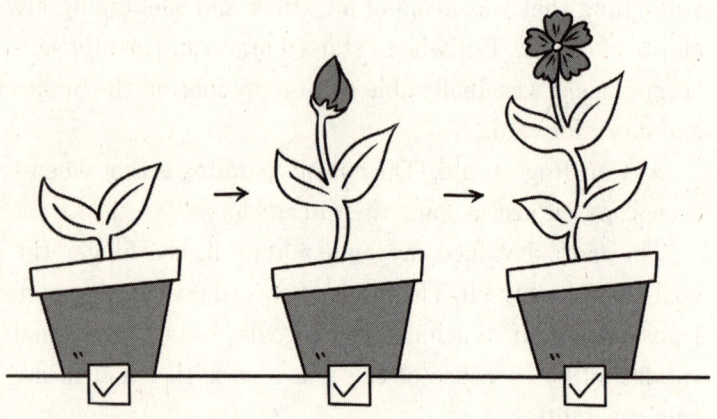

23

Day One or Day Two?

On novelty and meaning in everyday life

When you look back at the wonderful life you have lived so far, how many moments stand out in your mind?

I'm sure there are several important milestones that come to mind: birthdays, weddings, or other notable periods of celebration or transition. On the other hand, when you think of all the individual days of the year, you might notice a sense of sameness or monotony. Many of those days seem to collapse together into one big blur of time.

Neurologist Lila Davachi says, 'Time is memory.' In other words, we measure time not just objectively, with the seconds and minutes that go by on the clock, but also subjectively – with the memories associated with time.

What gives any unit of time – a day, a week, a year – fullness and meaning is having significant memories attached to it. The question then is: How do we create more memories to add to the richness of our lives?

It's difficult for the brain to process and catalogue memories when each day feels the same. The key is to add an element of novelty to our experiences – a sense of newness or adventure in ways big and small. In her book *Off the Clock*, Laura Vanderkam shares that you can do this by asking a simple, yet powerful, question:

'What is going to make today different?'

This simple act of introspection helps you become intentional about the little things that could make your day, or even your entire week, stand out for years to come. Can you reach out to a friend you haven't connected with in a while? Can you try a new restaurant or hobby? Can you take a different route to work today?

If you want to consciously create memories that you will fondly look back on for years to come, try this exercise.

As you go about your days this week, start each morning by asking: What is one thing I can do that will make today different?

24

Press Record or Fast-Forward?
On capturing meaningful moments

'Mama, remember when you said ...'
'Babe, remember that time when ...'

There have been so many times when loved ones have tried to get me to recall a moment from the past, but either I had no memory of it whatsoever, or my recollection was fuzzy at best.

For the longest time, I assumed I just had a poor memory. Then I started practising mindfulness and realized what I thought was a memory problem was actually an attention problem.

Here's the truth – the mind is not a faithful recording device. It doesn't dutifully store everything that happens in our lives. The mind only records what you pay attention to.

The reason I didn't remember all those moments with my loved ones was because I wasn't truly there. I might have been there physically, but my mind was always elsewhere. Sadly, research suggests that most of us miss up to 50 per cent of our lives because our attention is not in the present moment. Our minds are either off ruminating over past mistakes and hurts or worrying about the future.

You could be in the most gorgeous setting but if you spend most of your time on your phone, how much of that experience will you actually remember a year from now, let alone in five or ten years?

In her brilliant book *Peak Mind,* psychologist Amishi Jha explains that if you want to encode more meaningful moments from your life into your long-term memory, you need to get intentional about what you hit the mind's 'record button' for.

The next time you want to turn an ordinary moment into an extraordinary one, take a conscious breath to bring yourself into the present moment. Then lean into the moment by silently saying to yourself:

'Press record.'

Our memories are deeply connected to our senses. If you want to boost your chances of remembering life's special moments, use mindfulness to root yourself in the body in those moments.

You get a nice message from someone. Take a breath. Press record. Put your hand on your heart and express gratitude silently in your mind, allowing yourself to fully feel their appreciation.

You are enjoying a nice cup of coffee. Take a breath. Press record. Take in the aroma, savour the taste and soak in the experience.

Your child gives you a hug. Take a breath. Press record. Close your eyes, hug them for a few extra seconds and let yourself bask in their warm affection.

Each time you press record, you are slowing down and taking a conscious pause, allowing yourself to be fully present in the here and now, rather than letting your mind live in rewind or fast-forward mode.

At the end of the day, what you choose to focus on, savour and press record on becomes the fabric of your life.

My question to you: What are you pressing record on?

25

Avoid Boredom or Love It?
On boredom and mastery

Here's a question for you: What is your relationship with boredom?

I have a nine-year-old son. Every time I ask him to do some writing, his immediate response is, 'But that's so boring!' I lovingly reply, 'But doing boring things is important – it helps build character.' At which point, he rolls his eyes because he has no idea what that means.

My son is not alone in this. Many of us would do anything to avoid boredom. In fact, our need to escape boredom is at the root of many unhealthy habits. We endlessly scroll through social media to avoid boredom. We turn to junk food to fight boredom. At one point, I was a borderline shopaholic because I found the idea of re-wearing clothes ... well, boring!

A study published in *Science* found when given the option to either sit alone with their thoughts for up to fifteen minutes or administer an electric shock to themselves, 67 per cent of male participants and 25 per cent of female participants preferred to give themselves a shock.

Avoid Boredom or Love It?

The brain's preference for novelty may have something to do with this. Anything new and exciting gives us a hit of dopamine – the brain's reward hormone – so we constantly seek fresh stimuli. Even something negative is preferable over the discomfort of boredom.

Yet, paradoxically, doing the same things over and over again is exactly what leads to mastery. The more we keep avoiding boredom, the harder it gets to achieve the goals that matter most to us.

As Blaise Pascal said, 'All of humanity's problems stem from man's inability to sit quietly in a room alone.'

How do we build a healthier relationship with boredom? The first step is to understand what boredom is telling you.

According to boredom researcher, Dr Erin Westgate, boredom – like any other emotion – conveys valuable information. Just as anger might signal that an important boundary has been violated, boredom tells you that you are unable to pay attention to or find meaning in what you are doing.

And there lies part of the solution:

If a lack of meaning creates boredom, then articulating a clear sense of meaning helps diminish it.

Around five years ago, fed up with my overflowing closet, I decided to go on a complete clothing fast. I was determined to live more sustainably because it aligned with my overall mission to live consciously. At first, I feared this would be difficult to stick to. But surprisingly, once I connected the goal to a deeper 'why,' it became easy. I told myself that each day, each month, each year I went without buying anything new, I was forming an identity that I could be proud of – that of a conscious woman.

Once I did that, wearing the same shirt ten times no longer felt boring. It gave me a feeling of joy and fulfilment because of the meaning I attached to it.

The same principle applies to other areas of life. Doing taxes feels more meaningful when you know it's helping you sustain a high quality of life. Performing repetitive tasks at work feels less tedious when you understand how it contributes to the larger mission.

What if, instead of resisting boredom, you embraced it? What if you build the capacity to be able to sit and do nothing or repeat the same task over and over? What would become possible for you then?

Begin your journey of falling in love with boredom with this question: How can you attach a clearer sense of meaning to the things you find boring?

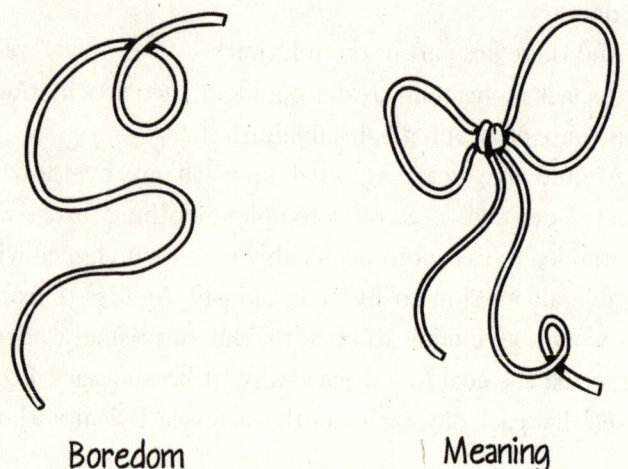

Boredom　　　　　Meaning

26

The Beginner's Mind or the Expert Mind?

On curiosity and learning

A student once visited a Zen master seeking advice. As the master began to teach, the student kept interrupting, sharing his own opinions and stories. Finally, the master suggested they take a break for tea. He started pouring some tea into the cup but he kept pouring, until the tea overflowed.

'Stop!' the student cried. 'Can't you see the cup is already full?' The Zen master gently replied, 'Precisely. You are like this cup, so full of your own ideas that nothing new can get in. Come back to me with an empty cup.'

One of the biggest obstacles to seeing things clearly – and to learning and growing – is a mind that is full of preconceived ideas, thoughts and beliefs.

Thoughts like: 'Oh, I already know this' or 'I know what they're like.' These automatic judgments make us jaded and can even rob us of our creativity and sense of wonder. The process of emptying your cup involves releasing these fixed ideas and judgments so that you can make room for new ways of seeing situations, people and experiences.

In Zen Buddhism, this principle is known as *shoshin*, or 'the beginner's mind'. It involves approaching situations with a sense of curiosity, humility and the openness of a beginner. A simple but powerful way to cultivate a beginner's mind is by replacing the words 'I know' with 'I wonder'.

'I *know* how this works' becomes '*I wonder* how this works.'

'I *know* what she is thinking' becomes '*I wonder* what she is thinking.'

'I *know* this place' becomes '*I wonder* what new thing I can discover about this place.'

'I *know* how this tastes' becomes '*I wonder* what makes this taste this way.'

As Zen teacher Shunryu Suzuki writes:

'In the beginner's mind, there are many possibilities. In the expert's mind, there are few.'

When you meet each moment with an open mind, detached from fixed expectations or strategies, you discover new possibilities. Allow yourself to experiment more, fail at times and create space for unexpected learnings.

Children naturally view the world with awe and wonder. As adults, we often lose this ability. But if we continue to look at things we think we already know with a fresh perspective and nurture our curiosity, we open ourselves to a world of possibility. As Marcel Proust so beautifully put it:

'The real voyage of discovery consists not in seeking new landscapes, but in having new eyes.'

The Beginner's Mind or the Expert Mind?

The questions I leave you with are: What is a problem, an experience or a relationship in your life that is calling you to empty your cup? How can you look at it afresh with a beginner's mind?

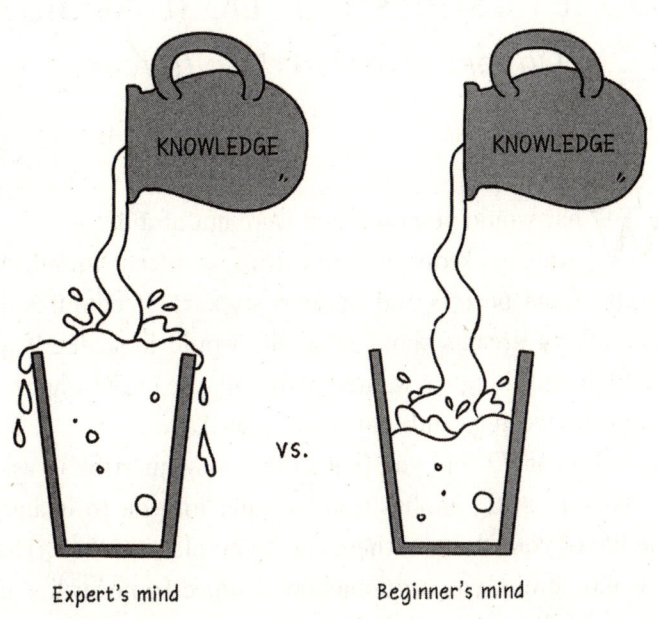

Expert's mind vs. Beginner's mind

27

Do It Fearlessly or Do It Afraid?
On taking action despite fear

What would you do if you were not afraid?

Such a seductive question – often found on inspirational posters and bumper stickers. It conjures up all kinds of dreams about what life would look like if we could do anything we wanted. After all, the only thing that stands between us and that life is ... well, fear.

But what if I told you that's the wrong question to ask?

This question implies that in order for you to imagine the life of your dreams, there can be no place for fear. That if you're afraid, you are somehow doomed to never live up to your fullest potential. This negative perception of fear creates a contentious relationship with both our fears ('Go away, you horrible fear!') and ourselves ('What's wrong with me? Why am I so afraid?').

But fear is among the most human of emotions. It serves a purpose. It alerts us to potential harm and helps us stay alive. The problem isn't fear itself – it's our fraught relationship with fear that stops us from creating the life we want.

Does that mean we should simply live in fear, instead of trying to build courage? Not at all. Courage is one of my core values. But we *can* build a healthier relationship with our fears – one that is free of judgment. We can strengthen the part of us that wants to be brave without denying, suppressing or judging the part of us that is afraid.

When you come from a place of acceptance, two things happen. First, you open yourself up to seeing the wisdom behind your fear and learn from it. In *The Hero's Journey*, Joseph Campbell talks about the central role fear plays in every hero's story. Fear tells the hero what direction to move in, because right on the other side of fear lies their greatest growth. As Campbell says: 'The cave you fear to enter holds the treasure that you seek.' In other words, your fears are telling you that if you move towards them, you will find the treasure or transformation you seek.

Second, you create a strong foundation for wholehearted living. This means embracing the full range of human emotions – the pleasant as well as the not-so-pleasant. Instead of thinking in binary terms – 'I am either afraid or brave' – you make space for both and say:

'Yes, I am afraid, and that's okay because it does not diminish my ability to be brave at the same time.'

Let's create a healthier relationship with our fears and adopt a more mindful approach to courage – one that begins not with judgment, but with acceptance.

The question I leave you with is not, 'What would you do if you were not afraid?' **but rather**, 'What will you do *because* you are afraid?'

28

Overcome Impostor Syndrome or Celebrate It?

On reframing self-doubt

If there is one feeling most of us have in common it's Impostor Syndrome, otherwise known as the voice of self-doubt.

You want to share your ideas, but Impostor Syndrome makes you question if you have anything useful to say.

You want to be more visible, but Impostor Syndrome makes you wonder if you are being too ambitious or overestimating yourself.

You want to reach out to someone important but Impostor Syndrome makes you question why they would bother responding to your email.

The other day I was feeling particularly anxious because I had an important speaking engagement coming up. My mind kept racing: 'Have I taken on too much? Am I good enough to do justice to this opportunity?'

Feeling like an impostor is almost always unpleasant. In that moment, I just wanted the feeling to go away. But then I asked myself:

When do we feel like impostors?

Do you feel like an impostor when you are safe and comfortable, sitting on the couch watching Netflix? Do you feel like an impostor when you are doing something you already know how to do?

No.

You only experience Impostor Syndrome when you are pushing yourself beyond what you are currently capable of.

In that moment, I had a realization – Maybe I was an impostor because I was trying to do something bigger than I had done before. But why was that a bad thing?

Instead of letting my mind's inherent negativity bias take over, I turned that thinking on its head. 'Yes, I feel like an impostor right now. But that can only mean good things – that I am pushing myself to go outside my comfort zone. That I am moving in the right direction. That I am about to attempt something that will help me learn and grow.'

Research shows high achievers are much more likely to experience Impostor Syndrome – precisely because they are constantly challenging themselves in new ways. For instance, a 2020 KPMG survey found that 75 per cent of female executives reported experiencing impostor syndrome at some point in their careers.

Feeling like an impostor? Congratulations, take it as a clear sign that you are a high achiever!

The next time you feel like an impostor, instead of letting that moment become a moment of weakness, pop the proverbial champagne bottle and ask: **What about this feeling can I celebrate?**

Overcome Impostor Syndrome or Celebrate It?

29

Desire A or Desire B?
On managing competing desires

We all have moments when we feel stuck – wanting to change something about ourselves or go after a certain goal, yet unable to move forward.

We know what needs to be done.

We're just not doing it.

I once reached out a coach to better understand a challenge I was experiencing in my business. I shared with her how one part of me felt I was ready to take a massive leap in my business while another part of me felt scared, and that this inner conflict was slowing me down.

She asked me a powerful question – one that I continue to come back to whenever I feel stuck. '*What are you gaining from not changing?*'

This left me stumped. I'd never quite thought of it that way but the more I reflected on it, the more sense it made. Clearly, I was deriving some benefit from the status quo which made me resistant to changing it.

Lisa Lahey and Robert Kegan, from the Harvard Graduate School of Education, explore this idea brilliantly in their book *Immunity to Change*. They explain that one of the things that stops us from moving forward with a goal is what they call a 'competing commitment' – a hidden, opposing desire that keeps us stuck.

One part of you wants to build your visibility and have a stronger voice. But another part of you is committed to protecting yourself from judgment.

One part of you wants to start a business and live life on your own terms. Another part of you is committed to protecting yourself from failure.

One part of you wants to collaborate with others and ask them for help. Another part of you is committed to protecting yourself from rejection.

In each of these cases, what you gain from not taking action is safety. You shield yourself from potential failure, rejection or judgment – but in the process, you also deny the part of you that wants to grow and achieve more. So what can you do instead?

Try this three-step approach to moving forward. First, practise self-acceptance. Recognize that part of you is simply trying to keep you safe. Don't be hard of yourself for feeling stuck.

Second, bring greater awareness to your competing commitment. What is the underlying assumption you are making about change? What do you fear losing or what negative consequences are you imagining?

Third, design a small experiment to test your assumption. Instead of making a huge leap, take a small step to test your fear in a low-risk way.

Let's say you want to speak up more in meetings. Your

competing commitment may be to protect yourself from any judgment that casts a shadow on your competence. You can then design a small experiment to start sharing your ideas in a safe space – such as smaller meetings with two or three people. See what happens. Gather data on how people respond.

Over time, you may notice that there is no judgment. Your ideas are in fact well received. Great! You have now gathered valid data points that challenge your existing belief. Repeat the experiment a few times – in gradually larger settings – until you build enough evidence to form a new, empowering belief – 'I can speak my mind without fear of judgment!'

My exercise for you: Identify an area of your life where you feel stuck. Now, ask: What am I gaining from not changing?

30

Zoom In or Zoom Out?

On gaining a better perspective

Are you better at giving other people advice than you are at taking your own advice?

This is known as Solomon's Paradox. In the Old Testament, King Solomon was considered one of the wisest men who ever lived. Yet, despite his wisdom, he struggled to apply it to his own life. His personal affairs were a mess – he was obsessed with money and was largely absent from his loved ones.

Sound familiar? Many of us are great at fixing other people's problems but struggle with our own.

Imagine this: a colleague is dealing with a conflict with another team member and comes to you for advice. Most likely, you'd advise them to have an open conversation to address the issue.

Now, if you were in a similar situation? You might avoid the conversation altogether because the idea of confronting someone makes you uncomfortable. Why does this happen? More importantly, how can you get better at solving your own problems?

The reason you can see another person's problem so clearly is because you're able to look at it from a psychological distance. Your colleague who is emotionally involved in the situation is stressed and can only see it from one angle – their own. You, on the other hand, can zoom out and consider the perspective of everyone involved. The ability to detach from just one way of looking at the issue allows you to be a lot more thoughtful and considerate.

The opposite happens when you are knee-deep in a tough situation. Your perspective narrows. The problem feels overwhelming. Your emotions distort your ability to think clearly.

But here is the good news – you can turn on your 'inner coach' and become just as skilled at guiding yourself in those murky situations by making a simple yet powerful shift.

Speak to yourself using your own name or the second person pronoun 'you'.

Instead of saying 'How can *I* deal with this?', I try: '*Bhavna*, how can *you* best solve this? What would be the ideal outcome for *you* in this scenario? What can help *you* achieve that outcome?'

I know it sounds a little odd, but as psychology professor Ethan Kross, author of *Chatter*, points out, this technique works because it creates the same psychological distance that makes us so good at giving advice to others

A second or third person perspective helps you step outside yourself, zoom out from the problem and see the situation with fresh clarity.

I encourage you to give this a try and experience the shift in how you approach difficult decisions.

My question to you: Next time you need to decide the best course of action, what is a powerful question you can ask yourself using your own name?

31

Be Direct or Set High Expectations?

On giving wise feedback

Does the idea of giving feedback make your stomach churn?

Even the best of us can feel hesitant when delivering tough feedback and rightly so. On the one hand, you care about this person and want them to do better. On the other hand, you don't want to hurt them or have them think badly of you.

So how can we deliver feedback with compassion and ensure it is taken in the right spirit?

Professor David Yeager of the University of Texas conducted a study with a group of seventh grade students who were asked to write about their personal heroes. He then randomly split the group into two and asked their teacher to provide them with feedback.

Group 1 received the comment: *I am giving you these comments so you have feedback for your paper.*

Group 2 received the comment: *I am giving you these*

comments because I have high expectations of you and I believe you can reach them.

Both groups were then given the option to reattempt the assignment. Only 40 per cent of the students in Group 1 opted for this, while 80 per cent of Group 2 – almost double the number – decided to redo their papers.

What's the difference? Group 2 received what is called Wise Feedback which combines two essential elements: high standards and assurance.

When you deliver tough feedback by saying 'I am sharing this with you because I have high expectations of you *and* I believe you can reach them,' your words are received not as criticism but as a well-intentioned push.

This approach leverages the Pygmalion Effect – the psychological principle that people tend to meet the expectations set for them. The second part of the sentence, 'I believe you can reach them,' instills confidence and helps build what Carol Dweck calls a 'growth mindset' – the belief that with effort, one can improve.

You need both elements because without high expectations, mediocrity will thrive and without assurance, growth will feel challenging. Together they form a strong foundation that can turn potential into achievement.

You can go further by adding two additional elements – direction and support. You might say, 'Here is something you can try differently. And if you fail, I'm here to support you.' This helps cultivate a sense of belonging, reinforcing their belief that you are on their side and they can lean on you if needed.

Many of us have fond memories of a teacher or mentor that pushed us beyond what we thought we were capable of. You too can play that role for someone by finding the courage to share wise feedback that includes these four key elements:

1. High standards – Set the bar high.
2. Assurance – Instill belief in their ability.
3. Direction – Provide guidance on how to improve.
4. Support – Offer encouragement and help when needed.

The question I leave you with is: 'Who would you like to support with wise feedback?'

What it is   What it becomes

32

Lay Bricks or Build a Cathedral?
On finding deeper purpose in work

So often we start new things – books, goals, courses or projects – only to quickly lose interest and move on to the next thing, then the next and then another. This cycle can feel frustrating and unproductive.

A mentor of mine would say, 'It's like beating water.' What happens if you beat a bowl of water vigorously? Nothing, absolutely nothing. You exert a lot of effort, but there is nothing to show for it at the end of the day, leaving you feeling stuck or unfulfilled.

If this sounds familiar, you're not alone. Many people struggle with self-doubt, wondering if they've made the right choices. The good news? You can break free from this cycle by getting clarity on what you truly want – and more importantly, why you want it.

One of the primary reasons people get stuck 'beating water' is a lack of meaning and purpose behind their actions. Every action carries two levels of meanings – a lower-level and a higher-level. For instance, a lower-level meaning behind taking a course would be, 'Oh, I'll get a new certification.' A higher-level meaning would be, 'This course will help me grow into a better version of myself.'

This concept, known as 'Action Identification,' was coined by Robin Vallacher and Daniel Wagner. It suggests that becoming aware of the deeper meaning behind your actions can influence how you view yourself and the things that you do.

Let me share a story to illustrate:

There was once a tourist traveling through Rome who noticed three men sitting around cutting stone. Curious, she asked each of them the same question, 'What are you doing?'

The first stonecutter replied, 'I am breaking down this piece of granite.'

The second stonecutter said, 'I am building a door.'

The third stonecutter declared, 'I am building a cathedral.'

The first stonecutter attributed a lower-level meaning to his work, while the third saw the bigger picture – a higher-level meaning that gave him purpose and motivation. Which one do you think derived more fulfillment from their task?

As Simon Sinek writes in *Start with Why*, 'There are only two ways to influence human behavior: you can manipulate it or you can inspire it.'

Every day we engage in routine or mundane tasks. Some may feel downright unpleasant like doing paperwork, filling out forms or tackling tedious chores. While the action itself may be small, it can take a disproportionate amount of mental and emotional energy to execute because it feels

Lay Bricks or Build a Cathedral?

draining. The key to staying engaged? Connecting your actions to a bigger purpose.

Instead of viewing accounting work as a frustrating task, I tell myself I am building my capacity to engage with discomfort. This self-narrative helps me show up fully, even for the things I don't necessarily enjoy.

My question to you: What is your cathedral story? What higher-level meaning can you attach to your daily actions to create a sense of purpose?

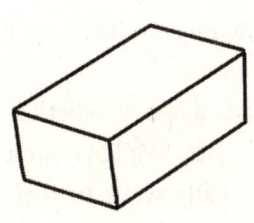

YOUR ACTIONS YOUR PURPOSE

33

Human Doing or Human Being?
On aligning decisions and values

There are many times in our lives when we find ourselves at a crossroads, forced to decide which way to go. Should I take the job or not? Should I marry this person or not? Should I move to a different city or not?

Often, these life and career decisions can be quite scary. The fear is always some version of, 'But what if I make the wrong decision? What would the consequences be? Can I live with those consequences?'

A few years ago, my family and I had to decide whether to move to Singapore. My first instinct was, 'We have such a comfortable life in Bangalore. Do I really want to rock the boat?'

One tool that helped me make a decision was changing the question I was asking myself.

Instead of 'What should I do?', I asked, 'Who should I *be*?'

After all, each of us is a 'human being' before a 'human doing'. Mindful living is about placing the being before the doing. And so, it helps to ask, 'Who am I being in this moment?' 'Who would I like to be in this moment?' 'What are the values with which I would like to show up in this moment?'

When I asked myself these questions, the answer was clear. I wished to be a woman who lives with courage. How would a woman of courage approach this situation? The answer again was clear. A woman of courage would do what is right, not just what feels comfortable. That is how we eventually made the decision to move.

That, and realizing that no single choice can entirely influence your level of happiness.

You could be in the greatest city in the world and still feel isolated. You could be working in an amazing organization and still be unhappy. You could be married to the most wonderful person and still feel a disconnect.

It's not the city itself but the many choices that you make in that city that determine your quality of life. It's not just the nature of your work but the attitude you bring to it every single day that determines how satisfying it is. It's not just the person you marry but the many micro-choices you make to cultivate that relationship that make it a healthy and happy one.

As Sukhinder Cassidy reminds us in her book *Choose Possibility*, the idea that a single choice can make or break you is a myth. In placing too much weight on one major choice, we forget how much power and influence we have to continually shape and re-shape our lives through the micro-choices we make every day, guided by the kind of people we wish to be.

So when you are facing critical moments in your life, I

encourage you to reframe your thought process from 'What should I do?' to 'Who should I be?' And then make the decision that takes you closer to becoming the person you aspire to be in light of the values that are most important to you.

Aligning our thoughts and actions with our highest values is at the very heart of living and leading mindfully.

The question I leave you with is: Who do you wish to be?

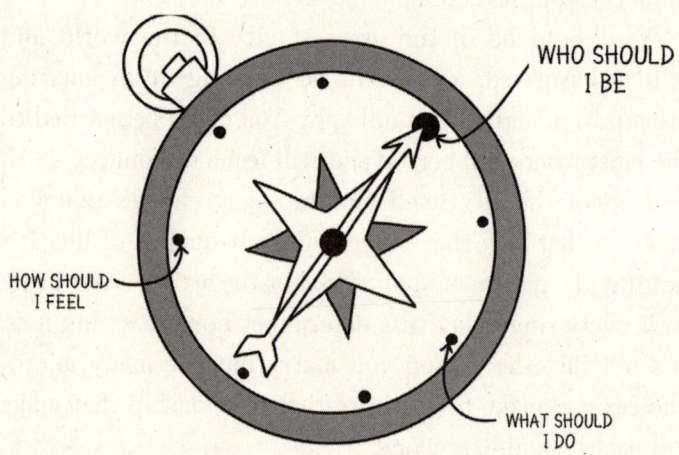

34

Procrastination or Progress?
On emotional regulation and action

Many of us have experienced the frustration of delaying an important project for weeks, months or even years. Whether it's writing a book, reorganizing the house or training for a marathon, we keep procrastinating, telling ourselves, 'I'll get to it later, when I have more time.'

As much as we'd like to fool ourselves, the truth is that procrastination is rarely a time management problem. Instead, as researcher Tim Pychyl notes, procrastination is an emotion regulation problem.

Let me share a personal example.

I first thought of creating a video series on living and leading more consciously back in 2017. When did I finally put my first video out into the world? Not until 2020. Why did I procrastinate for so long?

Here's what we need to understand about procrastination – each of us has a deep-seated need to be seen as both capable and competent, by ourselves and others. We attach our self-worth to our performance and ability. If there is even the slightest danger that our performance may indicate a lack of competence, we would much rather procrastinate and avoid the task altogether.

In other words, we often prefer the guilt of not doing something over the shame of feeling like we are not good enough. While procrastination may look like self-sabotage, it's actually a form of self-protection. We are protecting our sense of self and self-worth.

How do we get over this big hurdle? There are two powerful strategies that are helping me break free from this cycle (it's a work in progress!)

One, shift what you attach your self-worth to. Instead of measuring success by outcomes, focus on the process. I told myself to show up regularly to create my videos – which was within my control, rather than worrying about likes, comments or external validation – which were outside my control.

Russel Simmons wisely put it: 'Don't keep your eyes on the prize. Keep your eyes on the path.'

Two, make the task easier for yourself to start. Research shows that the pain and discomfort we associate with any task dissipates as soon as we begin.

Sometimes the mere thought of working on a task can feel painful. For example, one study found that people with math anxiety find it painful to even think about working on a math problem. But interestingly, as procrastination expert Rita Emmet found, as soon as those people started working on a math problem, their pain subsided.

Initially I had planned to create long-form YouTube videos, but that idea created a lot of mental resistance. So I pivoted to making short, bite-sized videos instead, which felt more manageable. And so began my routine of putting out a short video every Monday with the hashtag #MindfulMonday.

Ask yourself these questions: Are you procrastinating on a goal or dream that matters to you? If so, how can you shift your focus from the outcome to the process and make it easier to get started?

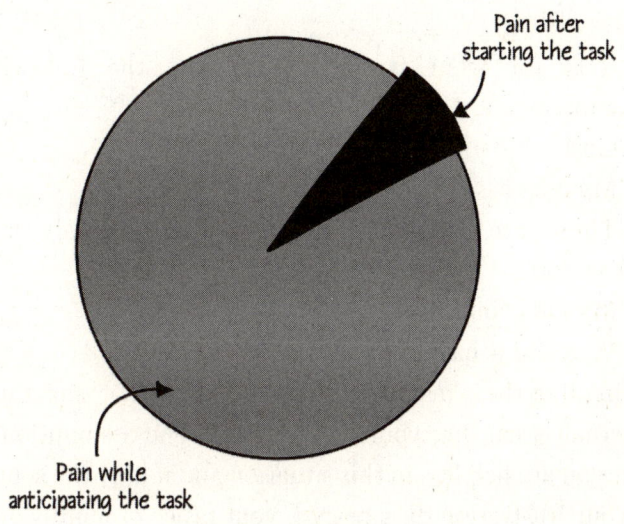

35

React or Respond?

On taking ownership of emotions

Look for what is common among the following statements:

'Gosh, this traffic is totally ruining my day!'

'My boss is so intimidating.'

'There are people on my team who simply lack motivation.'

'My kids don't listen to me.'

'Why did it have to rain today?'

In all of these instances, there is a belief that something external is causing your unhappiness. The assumption is that you are helpless in this situation and if only the source of your frustration disappeared, your peace of mind would be restored.

This way of thinking, however, gives power over your state of mind to others and external circumstances. The truth is, no one person and no one thing can have greater power over your state of mind than you yourself.

Rajiv Vij, in his book *Inside-Out Leadership*, emphasizes that the moment you take 100 per cent responsibility for your own thoughts, perceptions and behaviours, you start to experience a different reality - even if the circumstances of your life don't change.

Your response is your responsibility

There is no better example of this than Viktor Frankl's famous insight, drawn from his experiences in a Nazi concentration camp: 'Everything can be taken from a man but one thing: the last of the human freedoms – to choose one's attitude in any given set of circumstances, to choose one's own way.'

How can you create space for a more thoughtful response? Shift from reacting to responding. Shift the focus inward and reflect on how you can approach the situation differently.

Instead of: Why is my boss so intimidating?

Ask: Is my boss intimidating or can *I* exercise more courage in expressing my needs to him?

Instead of: My team lacks motivation.

Ask: Is my team the issue, or can *I* do more to inspire them?

Instead of: My kids don't listen to me.

Ask: Are my kids the problem or have *I* stopped listening to their needs?

This isn't about shifting blame from others to yourself, but rather about taking full ownership of how you can influence the situation. By doing so, you reclaim both your power and your peace of mind.

As the Dalai Lama wisely put it: 'When you think everything is someone else's fault, you will suffer a lot. When you realize that everything springs only from yourself, you will learn both peace and joy.'

Here's something to ponder over: What is currently bothering you? What conscious choice can you make to respond to the situation in a way that serves you better?

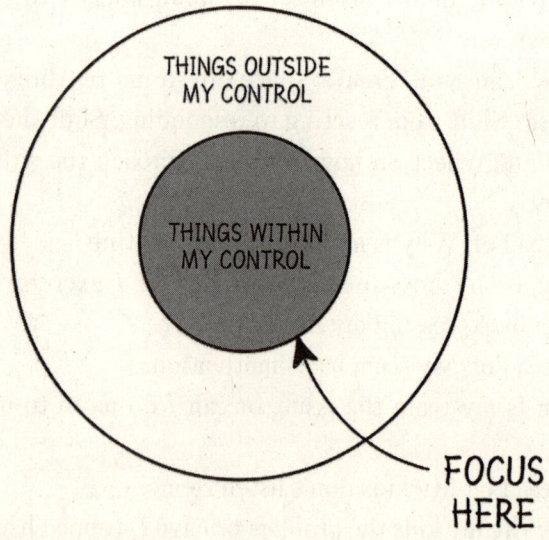

36

Positive Thinking or Negative Thinking?

On W.O.O.P. and realistic optimism

What's on your vision board? A powerful brand? Financial independence? A fit body? Travel and adventure?

What would help convert any of these dreams into reality? Most self-help literature tells us the key is positive thinking. For instance, if you want to lose weight, the advice is to visualize your dream body and imagine everything going perfectly as you reach your goal weight.

There is some merit to this – positive thoughts help you build the motivation and confidence you need to go after your goals. But it's often not enough to simply visualize your goals vision board-style. What if I told you that engaging in negative thinking could also increase your chances of success?

According to Gabriele Oettingen, a professor of Psychology at New York University, in addition to setting clear goals and believing they are possible, it is also helpful to consider the potential obstacles or challenges that could get in your way.

In other words, yes, have that beautiful vision board, but also stress test it against reality. Do this using a process called W.O.O.P.

W is for Wish. What is it that you wish for? For example, let's say it's a healthier body.

O is for Outcome. What is the deeper 'why' behind your goal? You want to have the energy to play with your children.

The second O is for Obstacles. What are the obstacles that could get in your way? A colleague offers you cake for their birthday when you're trying to minimize your intake of sugar.

The final P is for Plan. This is the most important. Don't just stop at thinking about all the things that could go wrong. Make a plan for what you will do if and when those pesky obstacles and challenges come along.

You could do this by creating 'if-then' implementation intentions, where for every obstacle you can imagine, you come up with a corresponding 'If ... then ...' statement.

Sticking with the same example, let's say you want to be consistent with your healthy habits. Your statements might be ...

'*If* I am offered cake, *then* I will enjoy a few bites without any guilt and get back to eating healthy.'

'*If* I start to lose motivation, *then* I will focus on making just one small change in my diet.'

'*If* I face judgment, *then* I will remind myself of why I am doing this in the first place.'

Positive Thinking or Negative Thinking? 109

When you make these kinds of 'pre-decisions', as Oettingen calls them, it helps you build both the skill and the willpower you need to overcome any obstacle.

This, my friend, is how you turn your dreams into reality with a scientifically proven method. Leverage both kinds of thinking – what could go right *and* what could go wrong – so that you are better prepared.

The questions I leave you with are: What is a goal you want to achieve? How can you W.O.O.P. it?

37

Safety or Punishment?

On risk-taking and psychological safety

At some point in your career, you have most likely worked as part of a team or several. When you look back, what kinds of teams allowed you to do your best work? Which ones allowed you to take more risks with your ideas?

A few years ago, Google ran a study to determine what their highest performing and most innovative teams had in common. They found a number of attributes, the top one being 'Psychological Safety'.

As Amy Edmondson of Harvard Business School notes, psychological safety in your environment gives you the comfort and assurance of being able to say, 'I know I can speak my mind or try new things, and even if I fail, I know I will not be judged or punished for it.' When you are in such a safe environment, you are much more likely to take risks and innovate.

We know extraordinary success or achievement doesn't come without taking risks – saying yes to new ideas, opportunities and responsibilities, even if they are beyond what you're currently ready for.

The problem is that while you want to take more risks, you also have a brain that is wired for safety and comfort above growth. Of course, you'd love to be more innovative or outspoken, but what can you do about that wretched fear of failure, rejection or judgment?

That's where psychological safety of a different kind can help. Just as it's important to create psychological safety in our external environment, it's equally important to create psychological safety in our internal environment – our minds. Often, it's not the people around you that are judging you. That critical inner voice can be the most punishing of all.

Here's what's important to note – your brain doesn't differentiate between harsh criticism from others versus yourself. Both external criticism and self-criticism trigger the brain's threat response – 'This is not safe. Be prepared to run or fight.'

In other words, the absence of psychological safety keeps you locked in survival mode and that's not when you do your best work.

If you're particularly prone to being harsh to yourself whenever you fall short of your expectations, those repeated attacks eventually condition your mind to say, 'Let's take the safe path. There's no possibility of judgment there, from myself or others.'

So how can you tell yourself it's safe to take more risks? Make a firm promise to yourself that goes something like this:

'I am going to push myself to take more risks and even if things don't go well – especially if things don't go well – I promise that I will not judge or punish myself for it. I will always pat myself on the back for showing up with courage before I even begin to look at what I can learn and do differently next time.'

This is self-compassion in action. As researcher and professor Kristin Neff notes, when you can relate to yourself with kindness during instances of perceived failure, inadequacy or personal suffering, that's compassion turned inward. Helping others be their best is compassion. Helping yourself be your best is self-compassion.

Create internal psychological safety with self-compassion, which will then become the very thing that supports you in taking more risks and attaining the level of success that you desire.

The question I leave you with is: What would psychological safety sound like to you? What can you say to yourself and others to take more risks?

Safety or Punishment?

38

Be Yourself or Be Your Best Self?

On evolving beyond fixed identity

Authenticity is almost universally considered an admirable trait. We naturally love people who are unapologetically themselves. Many of us believe we have an 'authentic self' – that if only we could be true to who we think we are, we would make the best decisions.

But is that always the case?

Your personality or who you think you are can also become an easy excuse instead of a valuable trait, whenever you want to justify not taking action, even when you know it could lead to a better outcome. You may find yourself saying things like:

'I'm not going to put myself out there or talk about my work. That's bragging and I don't brag.'

'I'm not going to have that difficult conversation, it's not like me to engage in conflict.'

'I am not going to ask for help, it's not like me to depend on others.'

'I'm not going to network, I'm more of an introvert.'

As Adam Grant notes, 'If authenticity is what you prize most in life, there is a danger you could be stunting your own development.' Simply 'being yourself' can sometimes keep you trapped in your own limitations.

Is there a better way to think about authenticity?

Benjamin Hardy shares in *Personality Isn't Permanent* that you are constantly changing and evolving. So to whom should you be true – the you in the present or the you in the future?

The answer: Be true to the vision you have of your best self in light of your highest goals and your purpose.

At the simplest level, your best self can be defined by the values you choose to honour, above all else. Instead of simply reacting, think about the ideal you in the future who is fully expressing the values she holds most dear. Step into that idealized future self and ask: What would the best version of me do?

If fairness is a value of yours, then it does not matter if you are shy or an introvert. If you see something wrong, you speak up.

If compassion is a value of yours, it does not matter if putting yourself out there and sharing your ideas publicly makes you cringe. If you think your work can serve others, you share it as widely as you can.

If kindness is a value of yours, it does not matter if confrontation makes you uncomfortable. If your feedback can genuinely help someone, the kinder thing to do is to share it.

So no, don't be yourself. Be your best self!

My question to you: What qualities and values of your authentic self do you want to be true to?

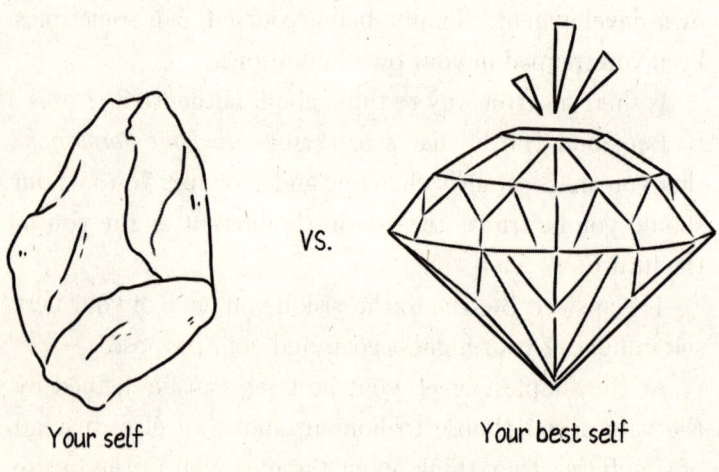

Your self   VS.   Your best self

39

Velcro or Teflon?

On training the brain for positive experiences

Everything you think and feel, enjoy and suffer, shapes your brain.

The brain is designed to constantly learn. It is always adapting based on our experiences. But there is one fundamental problem.

To help our ancestors survive in harsh conditions, the human brain developed a negativity bias, making it much more adept at learning from bad experiences than good ones. This makes sense – it was more essential for our survival to notice a tiger lurking nearby than a passerby who smiled at us.

As neuroscientist Rick Hansen writes, 'The brain is like Velcro for negative experiences and Teflon for positive ones.'

Imagine you have an appraisal discussion with your manager. He shares two positive things and one not-so-positive thing. What happens? The positive feedback slides right off, but the not-so-positive feedback sticks like Velcro.

You are left replaying the negative feedback over and over again in your mind.

This does not serve us well. If we don't stop to notice beneficial experiences – the moments of feeling appreciated, capable, or connected – we miss out on the opportunity to strengthen our inner resilience and sense of well-being.

Is there anything we can do to counteract this negativity bias and make sure the positive experiences also stick like Velcro? Absolutely.

The science of neuroplasticity tells us that the brain is malleable. You can choose to use your mind in a way that rewires it for the better.

Neurons that fire together wire together. In other words, the more you repeat a thought or action, the stronger the neural connection becomes. By consciously reinforcing positive experiences, you create new neural pathways that support a different way of showing up in the world.

How? According to Rick Hansen, here is the pattern of behavior you want to consciously repeat to create those new neural pathways: 'Have it, enjoy it'.

The next time you have a positive experience, slow down to notice it and savor it. Take five to ten seconds to stay with the feeling and allow it to fully sink in. The longer you stay with it, the stronger the imprint on your brain.

You had a random, pleasant thought about someone you know. Instead of letting that moment pass on by, pick up your phone and message them, 'Hey, I just thought of you.' It will make their day and yours.

You are hugging a loved one. Stay with that hug for at least five seconds. Lean into it, make it tighter and you might even close your eyes to feel the goodness of that precious moment.

You are enjoying a nice meal. Let the aroma and the texture of your food fully take over your senses. Savour every single bite.

If you practise savouring the good moments in your day as they happen, you allow your mind to settle into a state of calm and balance. Over time, this builds a reserve of positive emotions in the mind that acts as a shock-absorber when dealing with any negativity or challenges. In short, this makes you more resilient.

This is positive neuroplasticity – taking in and savoring everyday experiences to nurture inner strengths such as self-awareness, kindness and emotional balance.

My question to you: Which positive experience in your day, however small or ordinary, can you slow down for to practise 'Have it, enjoy it'?

40

Scarcity or Abundance?

On choosing empowering beliefs

How would you complete the sentence 'I am ...'?

Harvard University did a study with a group of Asian American women where half the participants were asked to check off their racial identity ('I am Asian American') before taking a Math test, while the others were asked to check off their gender identity ('I am a woman').

Guess which group performed better?

If you're thinking the first group, you are correct. Why? Because the prevailing belief is that Asian Americans are good at Math – internalizing that belief leads to better performance. On the flip side, since there is a bias that women are not as good at math, internalizing that belief hurts your performance.

The two most important words in the English language are 'I am'. What follows 'I am' matters – it matters a lot. It can impact your level of confidence and by extension, your performance and success.

For years I used to complete this sentence with everything that I am not, especially in comparison to others. 'I am not good enough.' 'I am not talented enough.' 'I am not lucky enough.'

I knew this had to change or I would never be able to make the kind of impact I wished to. As fate would have it, I took part in a powerful course on personal growth with a dear mentor of mine – Dr Srikumar Rao, author of *Modern Wisdom, Ancient Roots*.

Dr Rao told me, 'Bhavna, for the next ten days, I simply want you to find evidence of the fact that you live in a benevolent universe.'

I wasn't entirely sure what would come of this exercise, but as an eager and sincere student, I took him up on the challenge. Here is what I found over the next ten days:

Day 1, Evidence 1: I had been struggling to build my personal brand. While casually scrolling on LinkedIn, I came across a post from another leadership consultant whom I find hugely inspiring. This then sparked multiple creative ideas for how I could position my own brand.

Day 2, Evidence 2: I often walked past this antique furniture store near my house. Each time I would look wistfully at all the gorgeous pieces inside, but I could never justify spending that kind of money. As luck would have it, on day two, I saw a huge sign plastered across the store: 'Everything must go!' All their pieces had been marked down by at least 50 per cent. I finally entered the store and bought an exquisite console table.

Day 3, Evidence 3: Someone I had known a long time ago got back in touch with me to inquire about our leadership programmes for women. Long story short, our initial conversation led to multiple engagements with her organization over the course of that year.

And so it continued – day four, five and six ... Each day I sincerely looked and each day I found some evidence, however small, that the universe is indeed benevolent. I soon realized why Dr Rao had given me this exercise. He wanted me to find evidence that I am enough and that I will always be supported by the universe.

Find enough data to support a thought, and it will turn into a belief. Put enough conviction behind that belief, it will then shape your identity.

Could all of this have been a mere coincidence? Could you also find evidence that the universe is not working in your favor? Sure. You will find evidence for whatever you consciously look for. Precisely for that reason, why not look for evidence that helps you move through life with greater confidence and joy? As Dr Rao would say, 'You shape your world by what you observe.'

After all, every belief is a choice. Why not consciously choose the beliefs that serve you better?

Here is my question to you: What is an 'I am...' belief that you want to strengthen?

I invite you to do the same exercise Dr Rao gave me: for the next ten days, find evidence for why this belief is true. Stay true to the spirit of the exercise and I promise you will soon have a new empowering belief to reshape your identity.

Scarcity or Abundance?

41

Fierce or Tender Self-Compassion?

On balancing self-motivation and self-kindness

How do you speak to yourself in the moments leading up to an important situation that requires you to be at your confident best? Is your mind filled with self-doubt or encouragement?

How about after that moment of courage, especially if it didn't go as well as you had hoped? Are you kind or do you beat yourself up saying, 'Gosh what was I thinking? How could I have been so stupid?'

Here's the thing: how you speak to yourself matters, perhaps more than you realize. Without a supportive voice, you will struggle to find the motivation to consistently push your limits or to handle the inevitable rejection, judgment or failure.

What we all need to keep charging ahead in our journey of learning, growth and mastery is a generous dose of self-compassion.

What is self-compassion? Self-compassion is showing

yourself the same love and care that you would show to a good friend who is suffering. It's simply keeping your best interests at heart.

For many of us, a self-compassionate voice is unfamiliar. What's more familiar is harsh self-criticism. We avoid being too kind to ourselves, fearing that if we go easy on ourselves, we'll become lazy or self-indulgent.

This is where it helps to distinguish the two different kinds of self-compassion, as Dr Kristin Neff does in her book *Fierce Self-Compassion*.

Just as the Chinese philosophy of Yin and Yang talks about striking a balance between light and dark, positive and negative, active energy and receptive energy, Dr Neff talks about striking a balance between fierce self-compassion and tender self-compassion.

Imagine a friend or colleague shares with you that they are feeling particularly nervous about an upcoming presentation. Senior leaders are going to be present, so the stakes are high. What would you say to such a friend?

'You can do this! You are prepared for this. You are going to rock this presentation.'

Can you imagine saying the same to yourself the next time you are about to enter a situation that requires courage? This is fierce self-compassion. It's the kind of support we offer ourselves when we want to motivate or encourage ourselves to take action.

Now imagine the presentation didn't go as well as your friend would have liked. They got bombarded with tough questions in the end that they couldn't answer properly and are now feeling pretty lousy about the whole thing. What would you say to this friend now?

'It's OK. You did your best. Let's see what we can do to save the situation.' Or you might say, 'It's OK, you'll do better next time. Let's see what we can learn here.' You would, in other words, offer a lot of tender comfort to soften the blow.

Now imagine doing the same for yourself in your moments of perceived failure. This is tender self-compassion.

We need to cushion our moments of courage with both fierce and tender self-compassion.

Fierce self-compassion is what you use to share your voice and your ideas with the world, because you know they matter. Tender self-compassion is what you offer to yourself if and when those ideas are not received well.

Fierce self-compassion is what you use to make it to the gym in the morning because your health is a priority. Tender self-compassion is what you show yourself on those days when you simply don't have the energy to work out and need to rest.

Both fierce and tender self-compassion support you in becoming the person you wish to become and neither involve self-criticism or shame.

My question for you: What kind of self-compassion do you most need right now and how can you offer it to yourself?

42

Remember Life or Remember Death?
On living intentionally

Picture a jubilant crowd celebrating the victory of a Roman general who has just returned from battle. As the proud general moves through the crowd on his chariot, his advisor sits right behind him – his only job is to whisper, 'Memento mori.'

Memento mori is Latin for 'remember death'. The advisor is reminding the general that he will die one day and must not take this moment of celebration for granted.

After all, whether it's glory, wealth or happiness – it is all fleeting.

Ancient philosophers and wisdom traditions, from the Stoics to the Buddha, didn't avoid the reality of death – they embraced it.

The Stoics encouraged imagining that you have lost everything that you value – whether it is a loved one, your career, a physical ability or even your life itself. This practice helps generate a newfound appreciation for all that makes our life meaningful and prevents us from taking anything for granted.

They believed that only by acknowledging how short and fleeting life is can we free ourselves from the petty concerns of the day or obsessive planning for tomorrow. This perspective pulls us back into the present moment with purpose, where all that matters is you showing up as your best and most virtuous self.

Steve Jobs had a similar philosophy when he said, 'Remembering that I'll be dead soon is the most important tool I've ever encountered to help me make the big choices in life. Because almost everything – all external expectations, all pride, all fear of embarrassment or failure – these things just fall away in the face of death, leaving only what is truly important.'

Reminding ourselves that life is finite forces us to take a closer look at our goals and actions – the very things that consume so much of our time and effort – and ask: Are my goals fully aligned with where I want to end up? Checking to see if you are moving in the right direction is the first step to getting back on track.

Jobs, in fact, had a daily ritual. He would look at himself in the mirror and ask, 'If today were the last day of my life, would I still want to do what I am about to do today?' Whenever the answer was 'no' for many days in a row, he knew that something had to change.

Jeff Bezos, the founder of Amazon, developed a similar framework based on the awareness of life's impermanence. In what he calls the Regret Minimization Framework, you imagine your eighty-year-old self looking back at the decision you are currently deliberating. You then ask, 'Would my eighty-year-old self regret the decision I am about to make?'

This distancing technique is yet another way to bring clarity to what matters most. The purpose of the question is to minimize regret and make the decision that your future self would be most proud of. As Bezos shared, 'I knew that if I failed I wouldn't regret that, but I knew the one thing I might regret is not ever having tried.'

Here's my question to you: Knowing that your time is limited, what's one decision, however small, that you would make differently today?

43

Darkness or Light?

On overcoming fear to pursue dreams

Ask anyone you meet about their aspirations and you will find many who are holding on to an unlived dream. Why?

Because of the dreaded four-letter word: Fear.

Fear of failure: *What if it doesn't go well?*

Fear of judgment: *What will people think of me?*

Fear of rejection: *What if I lose my place (and the respect I currently have) in the community?*

Fear of success: *What if I am not able to handle the new demands this would entail?*

How do we liberate ourselves from the clutches of this dreaded feeling?

Here is one thing that is useful to know about fear – it loves vagueness!

When the thing that you fear is undefined and amorphous, this allows fear to grow. In the absence of specificity, the mind goes rogue and magnifies the perceived dangers and threats. Like Dumbledore says about Voldemort –

otherwise known as 'He Who Shall Not Be Named' – in the Harry Potter series:

'Fear of a name increases fear of the thing itself.'

What's the antidote? Call it by its name and the fear will diminish.

It is only when we turn toward our fears and define them as clearly as possible that we begin to take our power back. One framework that can help us do this is by Tim Ferris: Define–Prevent–Repair.

For example, let's say you are not sharing your ideas publicly because you are afraid of people judging you. Here are three steps you can take.

Step One: Define

Ask yourself what exactly are you afraid of? What is the worst-case scenario in your mind? Who do you believe will judge you? If they do judge you, what is the worst that will happen?

The very act of naming your fears adds specificity. In doing so, you reduce activity in the primal part of your brain that triggers the fight-or-flight response. Instead, you activate the pre-frontal cortex – the more rational part of your brain – so you can plan your response more thoughtfully.

As Yoda reminds us in Stars Wars: 'Named must your fear be before banish it you can!'

Step Two: Prevent

What action can you take to prevent the worst case scenario from happening?

Could you spend more time understanding what your

audience values, so your message or idea resonates with them? Could you improve how you share your ideas so they land better? Could you beta-test your idea privately with a smaller audience first before taking it public?

Step Three: Repair

If your fear does come true, how will you handle it? How will you repair the collateral damage, especially emotionally?

Let's say you receive some not-so-encouraging comments on your work. You might choose to ignore any detractors. You can choose to engage with negative feedback thoughtfully and defend your ideas. *Or* you can look at the whole experience as an exercise in learning, analyzing what worked and what didn't so you can adjust for next time.

The lesson here is simple: Pull your fears out from the shadowy darkness and expose them to the light of your logical and reasoning mind. You'll often find that what seemed like a tiger is just a tiny mouse you can easily handle.

In other words, don't avert your gaze from the things that scare you. Look them straight in the eye and march forward.

My question for you: What is a fear that is currently holding you back from a dream? How can you define it more clearly and take your power back?

The Conscious Choice

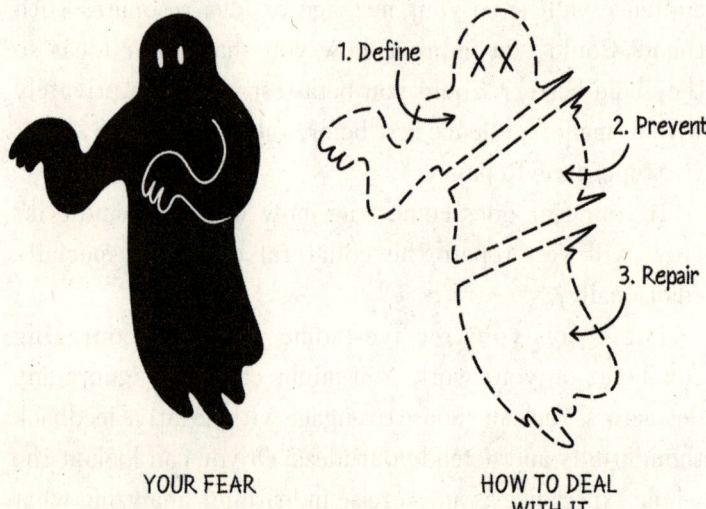

YOUR FEAR

HOW TO DEAL WITH IT

44

Wait for Good Weather or Dance in the Rain?

On taking action despite circumstances

'I'll do it tomorrow!'
'I'll do it when I feel like it!'

I'll be honest, I've had several moments where that voice in my head has led me to postpone important goals.

My gym membership expired. I found myself thinking, 'Let's renew it once I am done travelling over the next couple of months.'

That programme I wanted to launch before year-end? I found myself asking, 'How about we launch it early next year instead, when people are all charged up to invest in themselves?'

Those important changes I wanted to make in my business? I found myself suggesting, 'Let's make a fresh start next quarter!'

There's a problem with this line of thinking. It assumes we will live forever, that there will always be a tomorrow, that we can always make up for lost time. But is that true?

Here's a cautionary tale:

In June 1910, two expeditions set out from Europe with the goal of reaching the South Pole. One was led by Captain Roald Amundsen from Norway, while the other was led by Captain Robert Falcon from Great Britain.

The two had very different approaches to their Antarctic journeys.

The British captain pushed his crew to exhaustion on sunny days, while on bad weather days, they rested. The Norwegian captain and his crew believed in maintaining a steady pace so they sailed fifteen to twenty miles per day regardless of the weather.

Even when the Norwegian captain could see the South Pole and knew they could get there in a single day's push, they stuck to their steady pace and arrived three days later. On 14 December 1911, the crew became the first reported team in history to reach the South Pole, after which they safely made the 1,860 nautical miles journey home.

Meanwhile the British captain and his exhausted, demoralized team arrived at the pole thirty-four days late. Their return journey was even worse. Completely spent, all five crew-members suffered frostbite and froze to death.

The lesson is clear. You won't reach your goals if you only wait for the 'good weather' days. The days when you feel like doing something. The days when you feel motivated. The days that feel ideal.

Sure, we need days off for rest and celebration. But on other days, even a little progress – made consistently – can lead to big results. So, sunny or not, let's learn to dance in the rain, shall we?

Now, if you'll excuse me, I am going to go renew my gym membership!

My question to you: What is a goal you have been postponing that you can make a little progress on today?

45

City A or City B?
On location and well-being

My family and I recently moved to Singapore. Almost everyone who learned that we were moving here assured us that we would love it. I agreed. We *would* be happy here, but not because of anything inherent to this city.

The first reason I was so certain is best explained through the following story that I love about two men who visit a Zen master in a monastery.

The first man approaches the master and says, 'I'm thinking of moving to this town. What's it like?'

The Zen master asks, 'What was your old town like?'

'It was dreadful. Everyone was awful. I hated it,' the man replied.

'This town is very much the same. I don't think you should move here,' said the master.

The first man leaves and the second comes in.

He says, 'I'm thinking of moving to this town. What's it like?'

City A or City B?

The Zen master asks, 'What was your old town like?'

'It was wonderful. Everyone was friendly and I was happy. Just interested in a change now,' says the man.

'This town is very much the same. I think you will like it here,' the master replied.

I've been moving cities since I was six months old. Altogether, I have lived in eight different countries. In my childhood, we would relocate every few years because of my father's job. In the more recent past, it's been because of my or my spouse's work.

Right from childhood, I intuitively knew that in order to be happy in any city, I must find a way to fall in love with its culture, its cuisine and most of all, its people. I would actively look for reasons to fall in love – the more I would look, the more reasons I would find.

As Einstein said, 'The most important decision we make is whether we believe we live in a friendly or a hostile universe.' The innocence and purity of my young heart made me believe that we live in a friendly universe. Because I believed that, any part of the universe that I travelled to felt like home, and any city that I lived in gave me reasons to be happy.

The second reason why I was so sure I would love living in Singapore has to do with the science of happiness itself. As happiness researcher Sonja Lyubomirsky shares in *The How of Happiness*, changes in our life circumstances – including the city we live in – only account for 10 per cent of the variation in our level of happiness. 50 per cent of our happiness flows from a genetically-determined set-point –

a 'happiness set-point'. The remaining 40 per cent results from the conscious choices we make to think, act and live in a certain way.

These intentional choices include nurturing social relationships, practising acts of kindness, savouring life's joys, increasing flow experiences in your work and taking care of your physical health. Fortunately, these are all choices you can make no matter where you live, especially in the globalized and digitally connected world we live in today.

That is why I knew I would be happy in Singapore. I was happy in India and I will be happy in Singapore, because happiness is a conscious choice expressed every single day through all of your actions, big and small.

A question for you: What reasons can you find to fall in love with the city you are in?

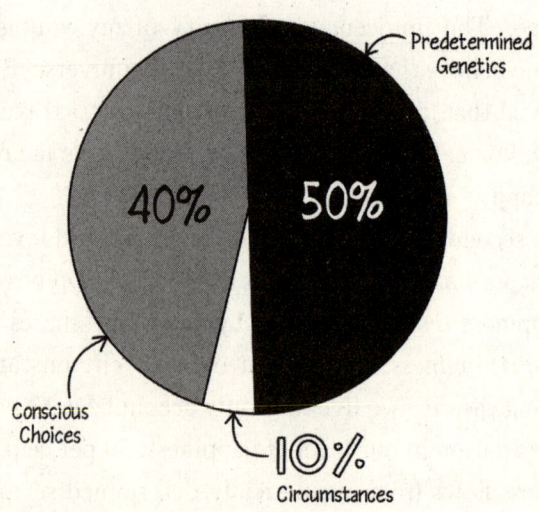

46

Be Normal or Embrace Eccentricity?
On celebrating individuality

A coaching client of mine once shared how she sometimes feels like a misfit. She felt sad and wondered if she would be happier if only she felt more normal like the people around her.

It got me thinking, why do we try so hard to be normal? Who decides what is normal? And why is being normal considered aspirational in a world where normality can be sub-optimal in so many ways?

It is normal to spend too much time on social media. It is normal to neglect your health. It is normal to overspend and live in debt.

On the other hand, it is not normal to wake up at the crack of dawn to train your mind for focus and calm – but I do. It is not normal to train your body for strength, week after week – but I do. It is not normal to live a minimalist life – but I do.

As Alan Cohen writes in *Spirit Means Business*,

What if being a misfit is not a defect, but a key to your success?

Maybe what you thought was wrong with you is what's right with you.

Just because you are out of the mainstream doesn't disqualify you from vast achievement.

You are in your own stream.

World change agents do not apologize for their eccentricities or try to hide them.

Idiosyncrasies come with the package.

Rather than suppressing what makes you unique, embrace it as a source of strength. Those quirks and unusual traits aren't flaws, they are signatures of originality. The world's most remarkable visionaries have succeeded not by conforming, but by leaning into their distinctiveness and using it to fuel their impact.

There are countless examples of great leaders across time with their fair share of abnormalities. Albert Einstein didn't learn to speak until he was three. Billionaire couple Narayana and Sudha Murthy prefer to travel in economy class. The Dalai Lama enjoys repairing his own watches.

Why not embrace your weirdness, your eccentricities, your oddness? Your unique gifts might be hidden among them – your non-conformity could be the very thing that leads you down a path to greater fulfilment. Instead of waiting to fit in, let your individuality shape the greatness you're meant to achieve.

My question to you: What is something weird or abnormal about you that you may actually want to celebrate?

Which key would unlock this lock?

NORMAL KEY   WEIRD KEY

47

To Give or To Take?

On generosity and relationship-building

To gain uncommon access to opportunities, ideas and valuable information that can help you advance in your career, it helps to have a strong network of supportive relationships.

I have found there is one quality, above all, that can work powerfully in nurturing these kinds of relationships in your network.

Become a Pain Detective!

There is a practical dimension to this, as well as a spiritual dimension. Let's begin with the practical.

Early in my career, I had to share a three-hour car ride to a work event with a senior leader in my firm. I was a junior marketer and he was the national sales director. I remember feeling incredibly nervous, thinking, 'What could I possibly talk to this person about for three hours?'

Fortunately, I didn't have to wonder for long because he had a string of questions for me:

'Bhavna, since you've been on the team for a while, do you have a perspective on this issue? What do you think about the processes we have in place? What do you think is working? What's not working? How do you suggest we fix what is not working?'

I decided to frankly share what the team's pain points were, in my opinion, and by the end of the ride, I had even offered to take the lead in addressing some of those pain points.

A part of me thought, 'Gosh, I have spoken too much. Surely I'm going to get fired now.' But the opposite happened. He was so appreciative of my candour and sincerity that after that day, he became my strongest advocate and supporter in the organization.

Research shows that having a sponsor – a senior leader who is willing to leverage their political and social capital to open doors for you – can be crucial to your career success. According to Harvard Business Review, cultivating such a sponsor, however, is a two-way street. While your sponsor can create opportunities for you, you also need to demonstrate that you are capable of detecting and addressing the challenges most important to them.

In other words, the surest way to attract a sponsor is by showing that you are a pain detective.

Now, the spiritual dimension.

There is not a human being alive who does not suffer in some way. We all have things we worry about – things that keep us up at night, that make us feel vulnerable. True compassion is when you genuinely seek to understand the struggles of others and take concerted action to lessen their burden. If and when you do, that becomes the strongest foundation for building a lasting relationship.

One senior leader I was coaching bonded with a prospective client over their shared anxiety about having daughters who were shy and struggled to make new friends. They arranged a playdate for their daughters, which ended up being a huge success. With that, their professional relationship began turning into a genuine friendship.

As Joe Polish, a passionate advocate of the idea of becoming a pain detective, writes in *What's In It For Them*, 'To be better at life and relationships, learn to ask, "How are they suffering, and how can I help?"'

So go become a pain detective! Build your network by focusing on what you can give rather than what you can get. The good news is, as Adam Grant reminds us in *Give and Take*, givers 'get to the top without cutting others down, finding ways of expanding the pie that benefit themselves and the people around them.'

My questions to you: Whom would you like to have a stronger relationship with? What pain do you detect in them that you can help lessen in some way?

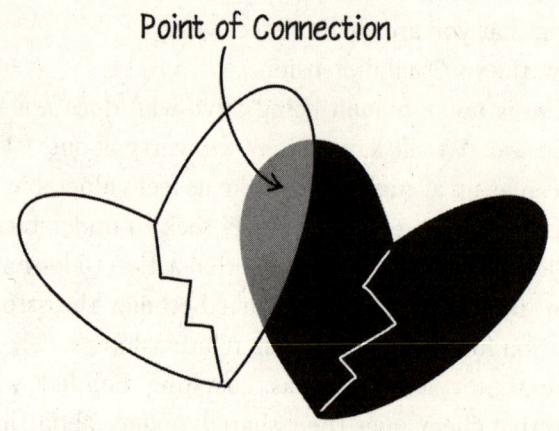

48

Give In or Keep Going?
On breaking cycles of self-sabotage

As a driven and goal-oriented person, you probably know the feeling of being 'in the zone.'

You are eating right.

You are getting your 10,000 steps in.

You are meditating and journaling every single day.

You are knocking items off your to-do list like nobody's business.

In short, you are at the top of your game!

But then, all of a sudden, something happens that breaks your success streak.

It's a party to celebrate a colleague's promotion and you help yourself to a chocolate cookie. It's just one cookie, after all.

Work was so hectic that you missed a workout, then another and another.

You experience an unexpected setback that shatters your peace of mind and now you just can't get back to your usual routine.

And then, you think, '*Oh, what the hell ...*'

'I had one cookie. I might as well eat the whole packet now.'

'I missed a few workouts. I might as well cancel that gym membership.'

'I missed my target for this year. Maybe I'll just write this year off.'

This is the 'What-the-Hell' effect and it can be one of the biggest obstacles in installing new habits and building a life that makes you feel proud. This phrase was originally coined by dieticians, but it applies to any setback in life.

So how do you break the cycle and get back on track?

You have two choices: Feel sorry for yourself and beat yourself up for falling off the wagon. *Or* exercise self-compassion and re-commit to your goals in a gentle way.

Make practicing self-compassion your conscious choice. Create a self-compassion message that you can use whenever you experience a setback.

According to researcher Kelly McGonigal, a self-compassion message has three components:

1. Being mindful of your feelings – Acknowledge what you are experiencing without judgment.
2. Acknowledgment of common humanity – Remind yourself that setbacks happen to everyone.
3. Encouragement over criticism – Instead of berating yourself, offer words of kindness and motivation.

For example, you might say something like, 'I feel guilty right now, but that's OK. We all make mistakes. Let me see what small action I can take to get back on track.'

In one weight loss study, McGonigal found that those

who practiced self-compassion lost twice as much weight and stuck with their diet twice as long, compared to those who gave in to the 'what-the-hell' effect and practiced self-criticism.

As a mentor of mine once said, *fail*ing is inevitable – at some point, life will get in the way. But *fall*ing is a choice. You can always make a conscious choice to rise above your failures with kindness, over and over again.

A question for you: What is a self-compassion message you can use to overcome the 'What-the-Hell' effect whenever you experience a setback?

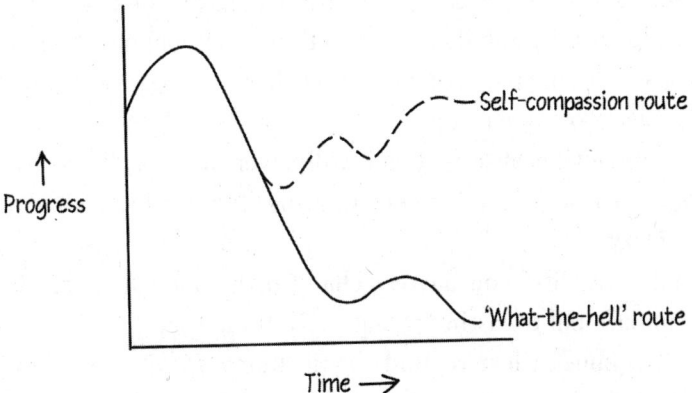

49

Change Outcome or Change Identity?

On identity-based transformation

Change is *hard*.

If you began the year with a long list of goals and changes you wanted to make and are now looking at your list wondering why you haven't made more progress, I want you to know one thing.

It's not because you lack willpower or motivation. It's not because you are procrastinating. It's not because you are lazy.

It's because you haven't changed the one thing that is foundational to lasting change – your identity.

As James Clear reminds us in *Atomic Habits*, there are three layers to behavioural change, each going deeper than the one before.

1. A change in outcomes
2. A change in process
3. A change in identity

For example, let's say you began the year with a goal to invest more effort online to build your brand.

Change Outcome or Change Identity?

If you said, 'I will be more visible on LinkedIn by posting fifty times over the course of the year,' that's a change in outcome – a specific result you hope to achieve.

If you said, 'I will devote sixty minutes each week creating content, without distractions,' that's a change in process – an adjustment in how you work toward the goal.

Now the question is: Did you also create a shift in identity?

Or did you continue to tell yourself, 'But I *am* an introvert. Showing up online and talking about my work feels like bragging'?

If you did, you likely struggled to follow through.

Instead, what if you said, 'I am a thought leader who loves creating value for others in my area of expertise'? That's a shift in identity.

One of the strongest forces in human psychology is the need to remain consistent with how we see ourselves. As Lanny Bassham writes in *With Winning in Mind*, how we behave will always be a function of how we see ourselves. Until you change that, nothing changes.

The University of California ran a study with two groups of pre-schoolers to see who would be more likely to help with chores and household tasks. For the first group, helping was framed as a verb or an action – 'Some children enjoy helping.' With the second group, helping was framed as a noun or an identity – 'Some children choose to be helpers.'

Guess who performed better?

The second group – the ones who identified as helpers! Why?

Because a verb is simply something you do. A noun is your identity. It is *who you are*.

And that, my friend, is the key to making a permanent shift in any sphere of life and career. It applies just as much to adults as it does do children. Don't just change what you do – change how you see yourself. Change what you say about yourself. Change what you believe about yourself.

Your self-image has been formed unconsciously, shaped by countless messages you've told yourself about who you are. The good news? You can consciously remake that self-image by creating new imprints.

Try repeating these five words: 'It's just like me to ...'
Complete the sentence. For example,
'It's just like me to wake up at 5 a.m. every day.'
'It's just like me to do deep work in the mornings.'
'It's just like me to take big risks in my career.'
'It's just like me to bounce right back after I fall.'
'It's just like me to practise love and forgiveness.'

Every time you show up as you aspire to – whether by taking action in reality or even just visualizing it – affirm your identity out loud: 'That's just like me!'

Make this your default mantra, a way to give yourself a pat on the back for every small step that brings you closer to your desired self-image. Over time, you will cultivate a powerful, unshakeable identity.

As James Clear writes, 'If you're looking to make a change, then I say stop worrying about results and start worrying about your identity. Become the type of person who can achieve the things you want to achieve. Build identity-based habits now. The results can come later.'

Change Outcome or Change Identity? 153

So how would you complete this sentence: 'It's just like me to ...'?

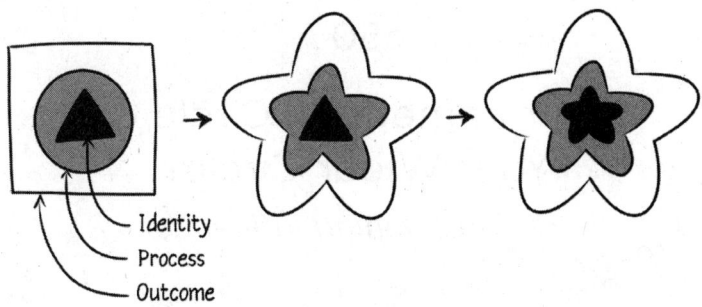

50

Your Immediate Circle or Your Wider Circle?

On broadening influence

Are you the average of the five people you surround yourself with most closely?

Many motivational speakers would certainly have you believe so. This idea is often credited to Jim Rohn, who famously said, 'You are the average of the five people you spend the most time with.' Another variation of this theme is, 'Show me your friends and I will show you your future.'

Except that's not entirely true.

Yes, your close friends, family and colleagues exert a strong influence on you. But that influence extends beyond just your immediate circle. When I reflect on three major decisions I've made in my life, none of them were directly inspired by the people closest to me.

First, I decided to leave my corporate career for several reasons, but a major tipping point was reading Tim Ferris' *The 4-Hour Work Week*. His insights on designing a lifestyle centered around autonomy and freedom struck a deep chord with me.

Second, my decision to become a mindfulness practitioner was sparked not by a close friend, but by a chance encounter with someone who had undergone a profound transformation after attending a ten-day *Vipassana* retreat.

Third, I made a decision to go on a multi-year clothing fast after I first heard of the idea from an acquaintance on Facebook, who had stopped shopping for a whole year.

Influence works in unexpected ways. According to research by Nicholas Christakis and James Fowler, if a friend becomes obese, you are 45 per cent more likely to gain weight. If a friend of a friend becomes obese, you are 20 per cent more likely to gain weight. And, if a friend of a friend of a friend becomes obese, you are still 10 per cent more likely to gain weight.

In other words, influence can ripple outward beyond your immediate relationships.

A person who inspires you to change the course of your life might not even be someone you know well but something about them resonates deeply with you. And that's encouraging news.

Even if your immediate circle isn't filled with the kind of people you aspire to emulate, you can still elevate yourself by expanding your sphere of influence. Surround yourself with great books, thought-provoking podcasts and a diverse network of people. You never know when a serendipitous encounter or idea might change everything.

So, be intentional about broadening your influences. Be willing to learn from anyone and everyone. And remember, you too may be impacting others in ways you aren't even aware of.

My question for you: Who are five people you would like to surround yourself with – even if indirectly – to evolve further?

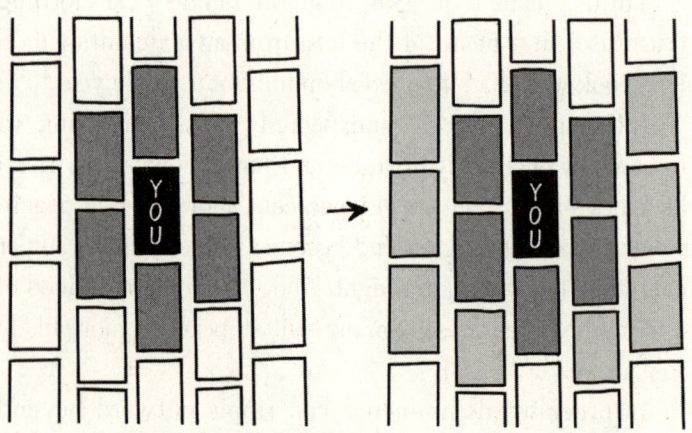

Expanding your circle of influence

51

Can't or Won't?

On the Power of Choice

There's a sneaky little four-letter word that has made its way into our thoughts and our language, often leading us to make choices that don't serve us well. That word is *'can't'*.

Let me share a few examples.

'I *can't* reach out to senior leaders in my organization. They won't have time for me.'

'I *can't* build a million-dollar business. I don't have the necessary experience.'

'I *can't* apply for that position. I'm not ready yet.'

The rationalizations we give ourselves sound quite convincing, don't they? And so the 'can't' remains a 'can't', leaving us feeling stuck, disappointed or frustrated.

But in my own experience, nine times out of ten, the 'can't' is really a 'won't'. It's not that we are incapable – it's that we are unconsciously choosing not to do something.

Try this quick exercise: Replace the words 'I can't' with 'I'm choosing not to …'

'I can't apply for that position' becomes 'I'm choosing not to apply for that position.'

'I can't reach out to senior leaders' becomes 'I'm choosing not to reach out to senior leaders.'

'I can't build a million-dollar business' becomes 'I'm choosing not to take the risks that will help me build a million-dollar business.'

Reframing your thoughts in this way is powerful because it shifts you from a place of helplessness to empowerment. It reminds you that you have a choice. Once you recognize this, you can do two things.

Step 1: Dig deeper. Ask yourself:
Why did I make this choice?
What am I afraid might happen?
Who or what am I trying to protect?
What is this choice costing me?

Step 2: Make a different choice. Ask yourself:
What would happen if I made a different choice?
Who would I become if I chose differently?
What would help me feel more confident in making that choice?

For example, instead of protecting yourself from possible rejection, what if you chose to apply for that position you don't feel ready for? What could help you make that choice? Would it be reaching out to a mentor who can guide you? Taking a course that helps you build skills in the areas where you feel challenged?

Can't or Won't?

We have the power to fundamentally change the quality of our lives with the choices we make, consciously or unconsciously. The key is to become aware of these choices and ensure they align with the life we want to create.

My question to you: Where in your life are you currently using the word 'can't'? What happens when you replace it with a conscious choice?

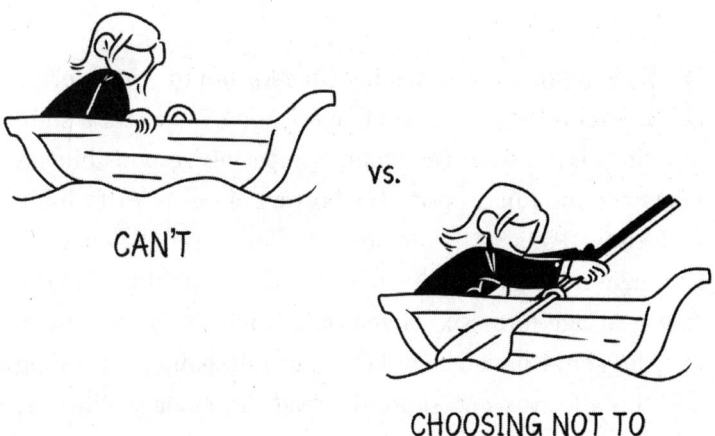

52

Choosing Fun or Waiting for It?
On making joy a priority

How often are you making time for fun in your life?

As children, fun feels effortless – it's our natural state of being. But as we get older, competing responsibilities take over and fun drops to the bottom of our priority list.

Randy Pausch, professor of Computer Science at Carnegie Mellon, was diagnosed with terminal pancreatic cancer at age forty-six. Given only three to six months to live, he could have easily fallen into despair, questioning why his life was cut short. Instead, he made a different choice.

He chose *fun*.

In his now-famous talk, *The Last Lecture – Really Achieving Your Childhood Dreams*, which has been viewed by millions, he spoke about how he used his remaining time to pursue cherished childhood dreams. Experiencing zero gravity, winning a stuffed animal at an amusement park and more.

His greatest lesson?

'Never underestimate the importance of having fun. I'm

dying and I'm having fun. And I'm going to keep having fun every day because there's no other way to play it.'

We do so many things in search of happiness. We work hard, chase success, accumulate wealth, believing that once we achieve these things, we'll finally be happy.

But in this endless pursuit, we overlook the simplest shortcut to happiness: having fun.

As behavioural scientist Mike Rucker shares in *The Fun Habit*, 'Unlike happiness, a subjective construct defined by human perception, fun is demonstrable, observable, real and immediately in our grasp.'

Research confirms that making time for fun enhances productivity, well-being and relationships. So how do we make fun an intentional part of our lives? To harness all these benefits and more, here are three simple ways to invite more fun into your life:

One, make fun a daily priority. Even small doses of fun can boost your mood. Whether it's taking a short break, dancing to your favorite song or playing a quick game with your kids, a little fun goes a long way.

Two, get creative. Turn routine tasks into fun activities by either changing the environment, whom you do it with or how you do it. For example, go running with a friend or do your taxes in a nice café while sipping your favourite beverage.

Three, schedule fun. While fun should never feel forced, blocking time on your calendar serves as a useful reminder for making fun a priority.

One thing we know for sure – our time here is limited. We don't need to wait until the end of our lives to make fun a priority – we can learn from the wisdom of those who've come close to death and made different choices. Instead of passively waiting for fun to find you, make a conscious choice to embrace it today.

A question for you: What fun activities or experiences do you want to make more time for?

53

Regret as Pain or Self-Awareness?

On learning from what could have been

Growing up, I loved dancing. I was happiest when practicing or performing, even if my only audience was my parents and the occasional friendly neighbourhood auntie. But somewhere along the way, life took over. My career took over. My family life took over. And dancing slowly faded into the background. I've always regretted not making it a bigger part of my life.

What about you? Do you have any regrets?

Regret is a universal human experience. There is no escaping it, unless you're living so cautiously that one might question whether you're truly participating in life at all. Studies show we are twice as likely to regret the things we didn't do rather than the things we did.

Do you wish you had made bolder choices in your career?

Do you wish you had followed your dreams?

Do you wish you had listened to your heart and not the expectations of others?

Since popular wisdom tells us to live with no regrets, many of us brush them aside or hold onto them for years – both of which can be unhealthy.

But here's the truth: Regret can be a powerful tool for self-awareness. As Daniel Pink writes in *The Power of Regret*, 'If we know what we truly regret, we know what we truly value.'

So how can we turn regret into growth?

Instead of treating regret as something to suppress, mindfully embrace it and ask:

What is my regret telling me about what truly matters to me?

One way to do this is by zooming out – detaching from the emotion and looking at it objectively. Imagine a close friend is experiencing the same regret. What advice would you give them? What action could they take to move forward?

When I applied this to my own life, I realized that if a friend was looking back at her lost childhood passion wistfully, I would help her find a way to bring it back into her life, even in a small way.

That's when I decided to start taking dance classes once a week. I may never become a professional dancer and that's okay. Some things in life are worth doing not because they lead to an outcome, but simply because they bring us joy.

You have the power to transform any regret into a story of growth, redemption or self-awareness. Instead of asking, *'What if I had done things differently?'*, ask, *'What choice can I make today to honor what I truly value?'*

You can always make a different choice today – a conscious choice. After all, as the Chinese proverb reminds us, 'The best time to plant a tree was twenty years ago; the next best time is now.'

My question for you: What does your biggest regret reveal about what you value? And what step can you take today to bring yourself peace?

54

Good or Bad?

On how we interpret life events

Have you noticed how often you wish for things to be different?

The other day, I paid close attention to my thoughts and I was shocked by how frequently I resisted reality.

I woke up in the morning and wished I'd had a better night of sleep. I went to my yoga class and wished my yoga instructor wouldn't make me do those dreaded backbends. I sat down to facilitate my first virtual training session for the day and wished more participants had their cameras on. After my son interrupted my session for the third time, I wished he would listen to me more. I ended my workday and wished I had more time left to fully unwind and relax.

By the time I went to bed, I felt exhausted. Nothing particularly bad had happened, yet I had spent my entire day fighting reality – mentally rejecting what was, in favor of what I thought should be.

As Michael Singer writes in *The Untethered Soul*, 'Suffering is caused by the contrast between what you mentally decided you want and the reality unfolding in front of you. To whatever degree they don't match, you suffer.'

The next morning, I tried a technique I learned from one of my favourite mindfulness teachers, Dr Srikumar Rao. Whenever you find yourself at odds with reality – or focusing on only one, often negative, aspect of that reality – say these words:

'This is neither good nor bad; it just is.'

Your judgement of a situation – 'This is bad', 'This should not be happening', 'I don't want this' – creates resistance. And resistance drains your energy. When you shift to a neutral state, you create space and allow acceptance, clarity and even peace to emerge.

The next day, I faced the same 'annoyances' as before. But this time, I applied the practice.

My yoga teacher made me do back-bends. I told myself, 'This is neither good nor bad; it just is.' I surrendered to the moment, and ended my yoga session feeling energized, with my mind, body and spirit fully nourished.

I sat down for an online coaching session with a client. My son interrupted me, once again.

I reminded myself, 'This is neither good nor bad; it just is.' I calmly explained that I was on an important call and would help him afterward.

My circumstances hadn't changed, but my response had. I ended the day feeling calmer and as the serenity prayer invokes, more empowered to change what I could and accept what I could not.

The *Bhagavad Gita*, an ancient Hindu spiritual

text, echoes this philosophy: 'Reshape yourself through the power of your will ... Those who have conquered themselves ... live in peace, alike in cold and heat, pleasure and pain, praise and blame ... To such people a clod of dirt, a stone and gold are the same ... Because they are impartial, they rise to great heights.'

Want to rise to great heights? Be impartial to the reality around you. Remember: It is neither good, nor bad; it just is.

My exercise for you: Throughout your day, pay attention to the moments when you wish something were different.

Pause. Say the mantra, *'This is neither good nor bad; it just is.'* Then ask: What is the best way to respond to this moment?

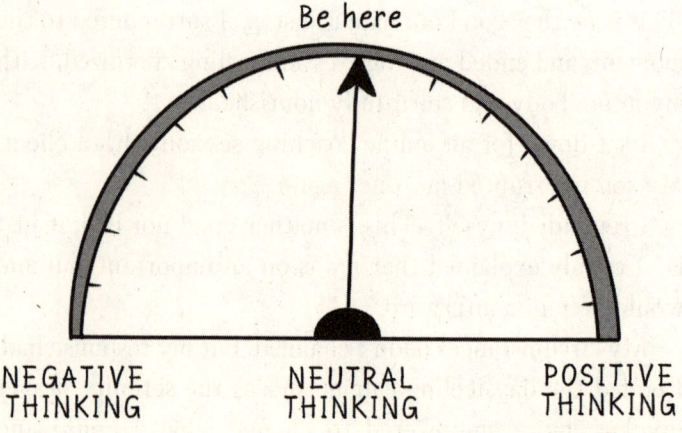

55

Fly High or Play Safe?
On the real lesson of Icarus

You've probably heard the famous myth of Icarus.

Trapped on the island of Crete, Daedalus crafted wings made of feathers and wax for himself and his son, Icarus, so they could escape. But before they took flight, he warned Icarus, 'Do not fly too close to the sun, or the heat will melt your wings.'

Icarus, overcome with exhilaration, ignored the warning. He soared higher and higher until the wax melted and he plunged into the sea.

For centuries, the lesson from this myth has been clear – flying too high is dangerous. Overreaching can lead to your downfall.

But what if that's only half the story?

As Seth Godin reminds us in *The Icarus Deception*, Daedalus didn't just warn Icarus about flying too high. He also warned him to not fly too low, or the sea's dampness would weigh down his wings.

Yet, society has conditioned us to only remember the first warning – the dangers of ambition, of dreaming too big, of taking bold risks. We are rarely warned about the dangers of flying too low – of playing it safe, settling for less and never truly seeing what we are capable of.

But any pilot will tell you that altitude is your friend. When a plane is high, even if its engine fails, the pilot has time to course-correct and land safely. But at lower altitudes, your options shrink.

The same is true in life. Playing small may feel comfortable, but it limits your possibilities.

As motivational speaker Les Brown puts it, 'Most people fail in life, not because they aim too high and miss, but because they aim too low and hit.'

Know that the true hurdle to flying higher is not a practical one, but a mental one. The key isn't reckless ambition. It's taking small, calculated risks and trusting that your wings will grow stronger with every flight.

James Cameron, legendary filmmaker of *Avatar* and *Titanic*, said it best: 'If you set your goals ridiculously high and it's a failure, you will fail above everyone else's success.'

Ask yourself: Am I flying high enough? Or am I holding myself back?

Where in your life are you choosing to play small?

And what's one bold step you can take today – to rise higher and trust your wings?

Fly High or Play Safe?

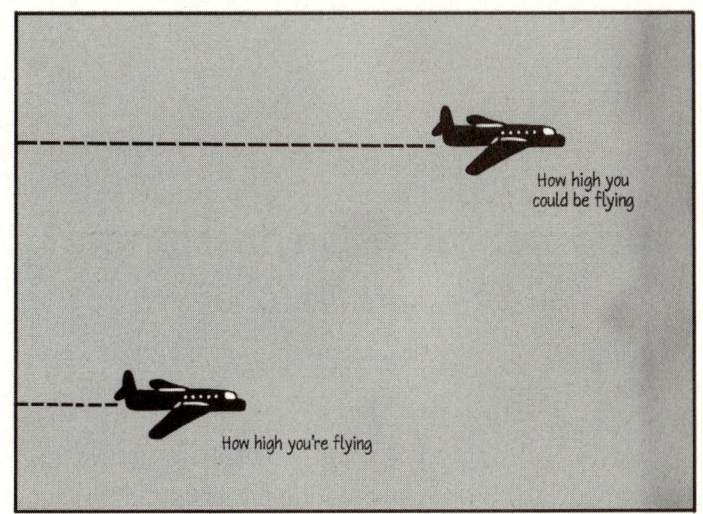

56

Judgmental or Dispassionate?
On navigating life like Google Maps

A few months ago, I flew into Bangalore and headed straight to conduct a day-long leadership programme for a group of mid-senior level women.

This was my first trip back after several months in Singapore and I had conveniently forgotten all about Bangalore's infamous traffic. Long story short, I didn't allow myself enough of a buffer to arrive at least an hour before the scheduled start time – something I always aim to do.

As I sat inside my Uber, I could feel my anxiety rising with each passing minute. Just to be safe, I switched on Google Maps for the last leg of the trip. At one point, it directed us to take a service lane. I missed the alert, which cost us another eight minutes.

Here's how the rest of the ride went.

Google Maps: Rerouting ...

My mind: Gosh, how could I be so careless? I should have paid more attention.

Google Maps: Take the next left turn.

My mind: Now I'm definitely going to be terribly late. What a disaster.

Google Maps: Take the next left turn in 100 meters.

My mind: Why did I even agree to an in-person session? Is this worth all this stress?

All along, Google Maps remained calm and dispassionate, matter-of-factly directing me to my destination. Meanwhile, my mind was spiraling – creating an unnecessary narrative of stress and self-judgment.

I finally arrived at the venue, twenty minutes ahead of schedule. The programme went exceedingly well, so much so that I was invited back for two more sessions.

Later that evening, as I reflected on my experience, I realized something powerful: What if we spoke to ourselves – and each other – the way Google Maps does? No, I don't mean we should speak in a robotic, monotone voice, though that would certainly be amusing! But what if, each time we made a mistake, we simply re-routed ourselves without the added narrative of judgment or ridicule. How much more peace of mind might we experience?

Imagine applying this mindset to other situations:

You indulge in a few unhealthy meals and feel off-track with your health goals. Instead of berating yourself – 'I have no discipline. I always mess up' – you turn on your inner Google Maps and say, 'Take the next left to your next healthy meal.'

A team member misses an important deadline. Instead of reacting with frustration – 'How could they be so irresponsible?' – you think, 'Okay, what's the next best route to get back on track?'

I can't promise that speaking to yourself with kindness and neutrality will get you to your goals any faster. But I can promise that you will enjoy the journey much more.

So crack open that window, let the breeze flow through your hair, turn up your favorite song and enjoy the ride!

My question to you: What is your next destination or goal and how can you guide yourself there with the calm wisdom of Google Maps?

Re-routing...

57

Student or Teacher?
On the best way to master a skill

Did you know that older siblings tend to have slightly higher IQ than their younger siblings?

I can almost hear the collective groan from all the younger siblings reading this!

The question is, why? Are parents investing more time in their firstborn children? Do they have higher expectations of them, which encourages older siblings to work harder? Do firstborns engage more with adults and as a result, learn more from them?

The most likely reason is that firstborn children benefit from something called the protégé effect.

Let's look at a study that will help explain this phenomenon. The Stanford School of Education split a group of eighth graders into two groups. One group was asked to study for a test as they normally would. The second group was told they would be teaching the material and that their performance would be evaluated based on how well they taught it.

Guess which group mastered the material better?

The group that was asked to teach.

Researchers have named this phenomenon the protégé effect – if you truly want to master something, learn it as if you were being asked to teach it to a protégé or a student. After all, as the great philosopher Seneca said, *'He who teaches learns.'*

We see this effect everywhere. Take medical students, for example. Studies show they retain and understand information better when they teach procedures to junior students rather than simply reviewing textbooks or notes. Even in workplaces, mentorship programmes don't just benefit the mentee; even the mentors often develop a deeper understanding of their craft and improve their leadership skills in the process.

And that is why older siblings often score higher on IQ tests, because they most likely grew up teaching their younger brothers and sisters.

So what does this mean for you?

If you want to accelerate your mastery in any subject or skill, don't just passively learn – teach it.

If you're learning a new concept at work, try explaining it to a colleague.

If you're developing a new habit, guide a friend through the process.

If you're building expertise in an area, mentor someone who is just starting out.

You don't have to be an expert to start teaching, you simply have to be one step ahead of someone else.

Student or Teacher?

My question to you: What's a skill or subject you want to gain mastery in? Who can you teach it to so you can learn it better yourself?

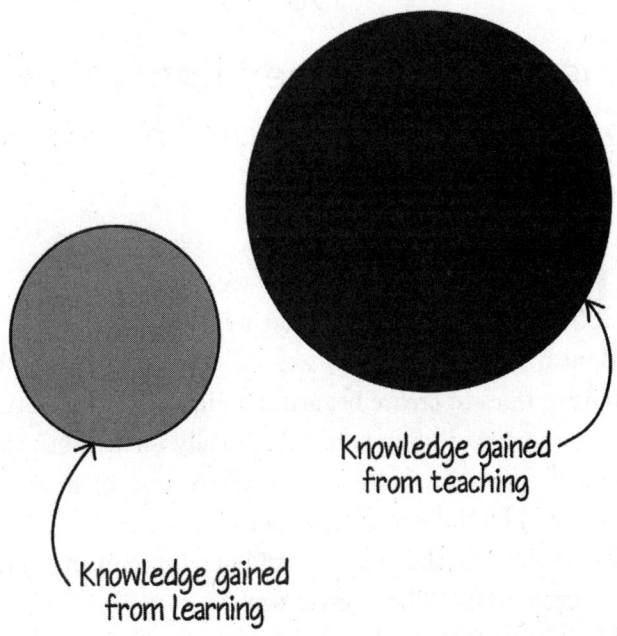

Knowledge gained from teaching

Knowledge gained from learning

58

The Bonsai or the Mighty Oak?
On breaking free from self-imposed limits

How do you contain a mighty tree? Simple: you put it inside a tiny pot!

Bonsai is the Japanese art of potting and shaping miniature trees to create beautiful, unique pieces of natural art. These trees, despite being genetically identical to their full-sized counterparts, remain small because their growth is restricted by the size of their pot.

But if you take the same tree and plant it in open ground, it will grow to its full, majestic size.

Similarly, a little fishbowl may keep a goldfish small, but place that same fish in a lake and it can grow several times larger.

Which got me thinking, what contains our growth?

What is that invisible fishbowl or plant pot that limits what you can achieve?

I believe our growth is often directly proportionate to the size and nature of our goals. Set a small goal, and you will only grow enough to meet it. Set a mighty goal and it will force you to stretch beyond your current limits, unlocking personal growth and mastery along the way.

The Bonsai or the Mighty Oak?

This is why I'm a big believer in setting audacious goals. Even if you don't hit the exact target, the act of striving toward something big expands your potential.

For example, I'm no longer shy about saying I'd like to positively impact millions of lives while building a thriving business in the process. Do I actually care about the monetary aspect of the goal? Not really. Do I care about the limits I'll have to push to achieve this lofty vision? Absolutely.

As Radhika Gupta, author of *Limitless*, shares, 'Only when you set your aspirations high will you push yourself to take the big leaps that can change your life. Sometimes life demands that you try to shoot the moon.'

And the good news is, unlike a Bonsai tree or a goldfish, we don't have to wait for someone else to move us into a larger space. We have the power to choose our environment by setting bigger challenges for ourselves.

So, here's a question for you to ponder: How large is the pot you are taking root in? Are your goals expansive enough to unlock your full potential?

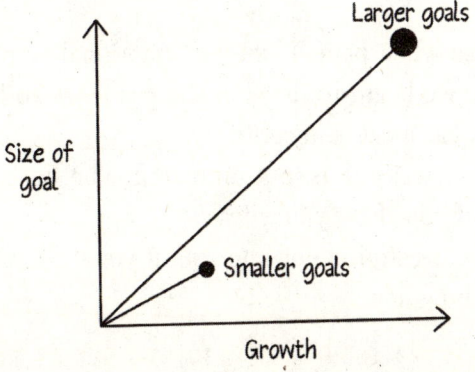

59

Pain or Uncertainty?
On what holds us back most

Imagine you are playing a video game with a friend. Your friend is told that every time they make an error, they will receive an electric shock. You, on the other hand, are told that every time you make an error, there's a fifty-fifty chance you might receive an electric shock.

Who do you think will be more stressed?

A 2016 study by Archy de Berker and colleagues tested this exact scenario and found that those who were unsure whether they would receive a shock were significantly more anxious than those who knew for certain they would.

Why?

Because when pain – whether emotional or physical – is certain, we begin to develop the resilience to handle it. What we fear most is uncertainty.

What's stressful is not knowing whether you'll be ridiculed if you share your ideas.

What's stressful is not knowing if you'll succeed if you try something new.

What's stressful is not knowing whether, if you tell someone you love them, they'll say it back.

So how do we deal with uncertainty? After all, you can't create a life worth living without taking some risks.

Here's a powerful way – create certainty anchors.

A certainty anchor is a ritual or habit that provides stability and predictability in your life. By creating a daily ritual or routine, whether it's meditation, exercise or journaling, you introduce a sense of stability to your day amidst all the uncertainty you otherwise experience.

For example, athletes often rely on pre-game rituals like visualization or specific warm-up sequences, to create a sense of control before stepping into high-pressure situations. Public speakers often have small certainty anchors – like deep breathing exercises or listening to a specific song – to manage nerves before walking onto a stage.

This has two key benefits. One, certainty anchors calm the mind. Our daily rituals give us something solid to hold onto, even when everything else feels unpredictable. Two, they act as shock absorbers. If things don't go your way, your routines provide a grounding force, helping you recover faster and regain control.

The more uncertainty you face, the more important it is to create your own certainty. You may not always control the outcome, but you can control the habits and rituals that keep you grounded.

My question to you: What is one powerful grounding ritual you are committed to practicing every single day?

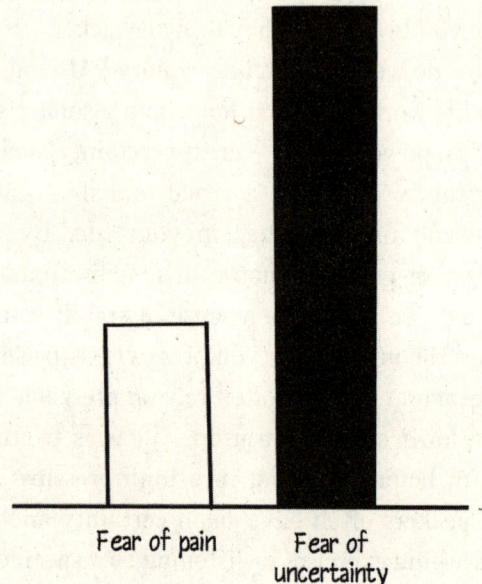

60

Confidence or Trust?
On keeping promises to yourself

If there is one almost-magical quality that most of us desire, it is confidence. We believe that if we were more confident, we could pursue our biggest goals, express ourselves freely and move through life with greater ease.

But what exactly *is* confidence and how do we build it?

The word confidence comes from the Latin *confidere*, meaning 'to have trust'. Specifically, to trust in yourself. This raises an important question: How do you build trust in yourself?

To answer that, let's look at the science of trust.

Dr Graham Massey and colleagues have identified two distinct types of trust that shape how we perceive and rely on others – cognitive trust and affective trust. Both play a crucial role in how we determine whether someone is dependable.

Cognitive trust is built when someone consistently honors the commitments they make to you. If a colleague always follows through on what they say, you naturally trust them more.

Affective trust develops when you believe someone genuinely cares about your well-being. If a leader's feedback is rooted in a genuine desire to see you grow, you're more likely to trust them.

Now let's apply both types of trust to building confidence in yourself.

To strengthen cognitive trust in yourself, make and keep small, realistic promises. Many people set themselves up for failure by committing to drastic changes overnight. If you decide to start eating healthier, telling yourself that starting tomorrow you will completely change your diet is unlikely to work. It is too big, too overwhelming and easy to abandon at the first sign of difficulty.

A better approach is to commit to something small and manageable, like cutting out sugary drinks for a week. That is an easier promise to keep, and over time, as you continue to follow through on small commitments, you start to reinforce a new internal narrative. Instead of doubting yourself, you start believing, 'I can do this. I've got this.'

To build affective trust in yourself, practise self-compassion when you falter. You *will* miss a day at the gym. You *will* break a streak. You *will* make mistakes. When that happens, it is easy to slip into self-criticism, but doing so only erodes trust further. Instead, acknowledge that setbacks are inevitable and recommit to showing up the next day.

As Alexander Pope said, 'To err is human.' What matters is not perfection, but consistency and self-kindness.

Confidence is built on two essential pillars. The first is integrity – knowing that you are the kind of person who does what you say you will do. The second is kindness – trusting that no matter the outcome, you will treat yourself with compassion. Confidence is not about never failing. It is about believing that no matter what, you will keep going.

If confidence is rooted in trust, then the question to ask yourself is this: What is one small promise you can make and keep to start building trust in yourself today?

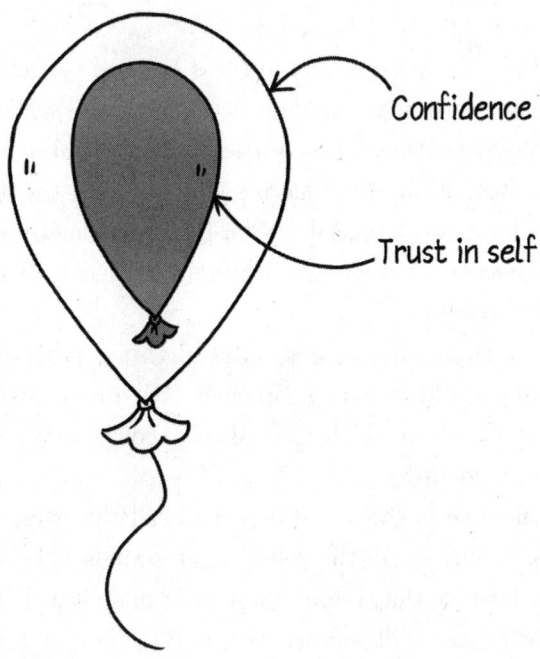

61

Confidence or Courage?
On what really moves you forward

We often assume that success belongs to those who are naturally confident – the ones who walk into a room with ease, speak up effortlessly and take bold action without hesitation. But what if confidence isn't the real key to unlocking our potential? What if there's something even more essential – something within our reach, even when we don't feel ready?

While confidence is a wonderful thing, I believe our focus on confidence is misplaced. We don't just need confidence – we need a healthy dose of courage. What's the difference, you ask?

Confidence is the voice in your head that says, 'I can do this.' Courage, on the other hand, sounds like, 'I don't know if I can do this. I don't know if I can do it well. I don't know whether I will succeed or fail. But I'm going to do it anyway, because it's important to me.'

This distinction is important. Confidence comes with experience. But the first few times you do something – whether it's leading an important project, speaking in front of a large audience, or taking on a new challenge – you simply don't have enough data to be able to say, 'I can do this.'

At that point, focusing on confidence is irrelevant. In fact, obsessing over your lack of confidence can stop you from taking action and lower your self-esteem, making you feel even worse.

What you need in those instances is courage. The most important question you can ask yourself to build courage is: How important is this to me?

Once you have a clear 'why', the next step is to ask: What is the tiniest act of courage I can undertake that will allow me to move forward?

You can then take that action. And another. And another. That is how, bit by bit, you build the courage to do the things that matter most to you.

Writing this book has been a massive act of courage for me. Was I confident in the beginning? Absolutely not. I'd never written a book before, after all. My impostor syndrome was having a field day, planting imaginary gremlins in my head, telling me that people would judge me or question my competence.

How did I get over myself? I reminded myself, repeatedly, of my deeper 'why'. I wanted to create something that could make a real impact in the world. Then, I broke down the process into the tiniest acts of courage. Create a rough outline for the book. Check. Write what Seth Godin calls the 'first shitty draft' for the introduction. Check. Write the 'shitty draft' of the second chapter. Check. Before I knew it, I had unstoppable momentum.

My true friend through this entire journey wasn't confidence – it was courage.

Let me ask you: Where in your life would you like to express more courage? Why is it important to you to show courage in this area? What's a tiny act of courage you can take toward your goal today?

Courage to Confidence

62

Alone or Together?
On finding comfort in shared humanity

When we go through difficult times, it's easy to feel like we are the only ones struggling. We scroll through social media and see curated glimpses of people's seemingly perfect lives. We walk into a room where everyone appears confident, successful and unburdened. And in contrast, our own challenges – our grief, our doubts, our fears – can make us feel isolated, as if no one else truly understands what we're going through.

But suffering is not unique to us. Pain and loss are woven into the human experience. A powerful Buddhist parable illustrates this truth beautifully.

Kisa Gautami's only child, a young son, had died. Devastated and feeling utterly helpless, she carried him from neighbour to neighbour, begging for someone – anyone to help her. One of them suggested she go to the Buddha and ask if he had a way to bring her son back to life.

Desperate for hope, Kisa found the Buddha and pleaded for his help. He listened with compassion and then gently instructed her to go back to her village and gather mustard seeds – but only from households that had never been touched by death. From those seeds, the Buddha promised, he would create medicine to bring her son back to life.

Relieved, she rushed back to her village and wandered from house to house, asking for mustard seeds.

At the first house, a young woman offered her some seeds. But when Kisa asked if she had ever lost a family member to death, the young woman said her grandmother had died recently.

She moved on to the second house. The woman who opened the door had been widowed a few years ago.

The third house had lost an uncle and the fourth, an aunt.

Kisa kept moving from house to house but the answer was always the same – every home had experienced loss. As night fell and she stood empty-handed, realization dawned upon her – no house is untouched by suffering

For the first time, she understood that she was not alone in her grief. And in that understanding, her pain began to ease.

Why am I sharing this story with you?

Because there is no house, no person, that is untouched by suffering.

At times, you may feel alone in your struggles. Perhaps you feel lost, unsure of your direction, while everyone else seems to have their life figured out. Maybe you're experiencing a painful disconnect from someone you once felt close to. Or perhaps you're carrying the weight of worry for a loved one's well-being.

Whatever your struggle may be, remember this:

Alone or Together?

Everyone suffers.

Everyone feels pain.

Everyone struggles in some way.

As Dr Kristin Neff, a pioneer in self-compassion research, reminds us, the very essence of being human is to be mortal, vulnerable and imperfect. Suffering is not a personal failing – it is part of our shared human experience.

In our most difficult moments, when we need self-compassion the most, it helps to affirm our shared humanity. You can do this with any statement that connects you to the rest of humankind.

'I feel guilty right now but that's okay. No one is perfect.'

'Everyone makes mistakes. I'll do better next time.'

'I'm not the only one who is struggling to figure out this thing called life.'

By reminding yourself that you are not alone, you shift from isolation to connection, from self-criticism to self-compassion.

My question to you: What is a statement you can use to affirm your connection to our shared human experience?

63

Turn Toward or Turn Away?
On facing difficult emotions mindfully

When I think about my future, part of me feels excited, especially when I consider the possibilities for my career. But I also experience a deep sense of unease when I think about my personal life. With my parents aging, I worry about what might happen if their health continues to decline.

It's normal to feel anxiety about the future, especially when so much of it is uncertain and out of our control. In fact, anxiety is a function of our brain's most primal survival instinct – its constant effort to predict the future and keep us safe. When the brain lacks enough information to confidently anticipate what lies ahead, we experience anxiety.

So, what can we do when difficult emotions arise?

Here's a simple but powerful practice that I find to be helpful whenever I am feeling anxious. Known as R.A.I.N., it offers a way to navigate emotions with greater awareness and self-compassion. Developed by psychologist and meditation teacher Tara Brach, this method provides a structured approach to working through difficult feelings.

R for **Recognizing** what you are experiencing.

The first step is to name the emotion you are feeling. According to psychologist Dr Joan Rosenberg, there are eight core emotions that most of us find unpleasant: anger, disappointment, embarrassment, frustration, helplessness, sadness, shame and vulnerability.

Research shows that simply naming an emotion can reduce its intensity. When you label a feeling – *I am anxious right now* or *I am feeling frustrated* – it shifts brain activity away from the emotional center (the limbic system) and engages the rational part of the brain (the prefrontal cortex), allowing you to respond more thoughtfully.

A for **Allowing** whatever it is that you are feeling.

When unpleasant emotions arise, we often try to resist or numb them by mindlessly scrolling through social media, binge-watching TV or distracting ourselves in other ways. But resisting emotions doesn't make them go away – in fact, it can make them stronger.

Instead, try allowing yourself to experience the feeling without judgment. Neuroscientist Dr Jill Bolte Taylor found that the life cycle of any emotion – no matter how intense – is surprisingly short. If you simply allow an emotion to arise and pass without resistance, it will typically dissipate within ninety seconds as your body naturally returns to balance.

I for **Investigating with curiosity**.

Where do you feel this emotion in your body? Is there a tightness in your stomach? A heaviness in your chest? A lump in your throat?

Instead of getting lost in overthinking, try shifting your attention to the physical sensations the emotion creates. This practice helps anchor you in the present moment, preventing your mind from spiraling into worst-case scenarios.

N for **Nurturing** yourself with kindness.

Finally, ask yourself: *What do I need right now?* Do you need to take a few deep breaths? Step outside for fresh air? Journal your thoughts? Call a friend?

Dr Kristin Neff suggests that offering ourselves the same kindness we would extend to a loved one is one of the most powerful ways to regulate difficult emotions. Sometimes, simply placing a hand over your heart and silently saying, *'It's okay. This is hard, but I'm here for myself'* can be enough to create a sense of comfort and resilience.

The next time you feel anxious, frustrated or overwhelmed, remember that you don't have to fight or suppress your emotions. Instead, try using the R.A.I.N method to mindfully turn toward them with awareness, acceptance and self-compassion.

My question to you: What is an unpleasant emotion you tend to avoid? How can you practise turning toward it instead of pushing it away?

64

Think More or Think Less?
On quieting the mind for clarity

From an early age, we are taught that success hinges on our ability to think – to think critically, to think creatively, to think outside the box. Later, in our work lives, we encounter even more variations like design thinking, strategic thinking, divergent thinking ... you name it, the list is endless. Thinking is seen as the ultimate tool for solving problems and achieving success.

But what if the real key to thinking better is learning how to think *less*?

We have an average of 70,000 thoughts a day, a majority of which, research suggests, don't really serve a purpose. Many are thoughts we simply rehash repeatedly in our minds. Psychologist Ethan Kross, author of *Chatter*, estimates that we talk to ourselves at a rate of 4,000 words per minute. That's a lot of noise to carry around in our minds, which – especially in times of stress – can negatively impact both our performance and well-being.

So how do we quiet the noise in our minds?

One of the most effective ways is not to think *harder*

Think More or Think Less?

but to redirect our attention to the body, specifically to the breath.

As science journalist James Nestor explains in *Breath*, most of us engage in quick, shallow and unfocused breathing. This contributes to a whole host of problems including anxiety, depression and high blood pressure. However, modern science – and ancient wisdom – reveal that controlling our breath can dramatically improve mental clarity, emotional regulation and overall well-being.

Recent studies have identified a 'perfect breath' – a simple breathing pattern that activates the body's relaxation response. This is a cycle of approximately eleven seconds – inhale for 5.5 seconds, then exhale for 5.5 seconds.

Let's try this. Sit comfortably and straighten your back. Breathe in slowly through your nose. Count to five: one... two... three... four... five. Hold for a moment. Exhale gently through your nose. Count down: five... four... three... two... one. Repeat for a few cycles.

That's a perfect breath. It's a rhythm of about six breaths per minute, as compared to the average of sixteen breaths that a typical resting adult takes per minute. Research by Dr Donald Noble of Emory University shows that this breathing pattern triggers a relaxation response in the body. Slower, longer breathing activates the parasympathetic nervous system, which helps you feel calmer. And when you are calmer, you think better.

Interestingly, this breathing rhythm is not new. It has been observed across various spiritual traditions – the Ave Maria prayers in Christianity, the chanting of yogic mantras in Hinduism and the rhythmic breathing of Buddhist meditation.

Both science and spirituality seem to agree – when we control our breath, we quiet the mind.

If you ever feel overwhelmed by your thoughts, remember: *You don't need to think harder, you need to breathe better.*

Instead of overanalyzing, pause. Take a deep, controlled breath. And with each slow inhale and exhale, create space for clarity, focus and peace.

The question I leave you with is: What is the quality of your breathing right now? How can you practise 'the perfect breath' a few times a day?

Inhale. Exhale.

65

Success or People?

On what truly brings happiness

What makes you happy? Seriously, take a moment to think about it.

We often tell ourselves things like, 'If only I were more successful, I'd be happier,' or 'If only I had the time and space to explore my passions, I'd be happier.' But can you be sure that achieving these things would truly bring lasting happiness?

For decades, researchers have attempted to answer the age-old question: What is the secret to happiness? One of the most compelling answers comes from the longest-running longitudinal study on happiness – Harvard University's Study of Adult Development.

For over eighty years, researchers have followed the same group of participants, tracking their physical and mental health. The study has uncovered valuable insights into what truly sustains well-being over a lifetime.

According to Robert Waldinger, the study's director, 'The surprising finding is that our relationships and how happy we are in our relationships, have a powerful influence on our health ... Taking care of your body is important, but tending to your relationships is a form of self-care too. That, I think, is the revelation.'

In other words, more than money, fame, social class or IQ, the best predictor of happiness and well-being is the quality of our relationships.

If relationships are central to happiness, how do we nurture and strengthen them?

Think about a time when you were speaking to someone, but even though they were physically present, you could tell they weren't really listening. Maybe they were distracted, checking their phone, glancing around the room or waiting for their turn to speak.

Now recall a moment when someone listened to you fully and attentively, creating a warm and encouraging space where you felt heard, without feeling rushed or judged.

The biggest gift we can give others is our presence. And one of the simplest ways to do that is through mindful listening with the intent to understand; with openness, curiosity and kindness.

Three simple words that can instantly convey to someone that you are truly listening – 'Tell me more.'

A friend comes to you with a problem? 'Tell me more. How are you feeling about this?'

A colleague shares an idea? 'That sounds interesting. Tell me more.'

A loved one is recounting their day? 'Tell me more. What happened next?'

These three magical words tell the other person: *I'm here. I'm listening. I care.*

The next time you're in a conversation, resist the urge to interrupt or get distracted. Instead, pause, focus fully and say, 'Tell me more.'

Who in your life could you try this with today?

66

Lucky or Unlucky?

On creating your own luck

Do you believe you are lucky or not-so-lucky? How you answer this question may be more revealing than you think.

I find the concept of luck fascinating. Some of history's greatest thinkers have spoken about it. Not as a mysterious force outside our control, but as something we can cultivate.

Seneca believed, 'Luck is what happens when preparation meets opportunity.'

Epicurus warned, 'It is folly for a man to pray to the gods for that which he has the power to obtain by himself.'

Machiavelli said, 'Fortune is like a river: if you build dikes and prepare for floods, you can channel its course.'

What if luck isn't something that happens to us, but something we generate? What if believing you're lucky actually makes you lucky?

Psychologist Richard Wiseman explores this very question in *The Luck Factor*, a study of why some people seem to experience good fortune consistently, while others struggle with bad luck. His hypothesis was simple yet powerful:

Our thoughts and behaviors shape our luck.

To test this, he conducted a study with 400 participants, half of whom identified as lucky, the other half as unlucky. In one experiment, he handed each participant a newspaper and asked them to count the number of photographs inside.

The unlucky group took an average of two minutes to complete the task. The lucky group? Just a few seconds.

Why?

Because on page two, there was a large, bold message that read: 'Stop counting. There are forty-three photographs in this newspaper.'

Midway through, another message offered: 'Stop counting, tell the experimenter you have seen this and win $250.'

The lucky people spotted these messages. They stopped counting, responded accordingly and even collected a cash prize. The unlucky people, however, either missed the signs or ignored them, too focused on the task at hand.

Both groups had the same opportunities. The only difference? The lucky ones noticed them.

Luck isn't just about chance – it's about exposure. The more you put yourself in situations where good things *could* happen, the more likely they *will* happen.

Sahil Bloom, author of *The 5 Types of Wealth,* refers to this as your 'luck surface area' – the space where lucky events can strike.

Sure, some factors are beyond our control: *where* we're born, *who* we're born to or unexpected life events. But beyond these, our actions, behaviors and mindset can either expand or shrink our luck surface area.

The Conscious Choice

In Dr Wiseman's study, the lucky participants actively increased their exposure to opportunities: They took different routes to work to meet new people and experience new things. They intentionally engaged with a diverse set of people at events and social gatherings. They maintained an open, optimistic mindset, even when things didn't go their way.

All this to say, luck is a choice. A conscious choice.

If you want to expand your luck surface area, take more chances. Meet new people. Share your ideas. Step outside your comfort zone. Speak up in that meeting. Say yes to an unexpected opportunity. You never know what it might lead to.

Because luck isn't something that happens to us; it's something we cultivate, one choice at a time.

My question to you: What is one action you can take today to increase your luck?

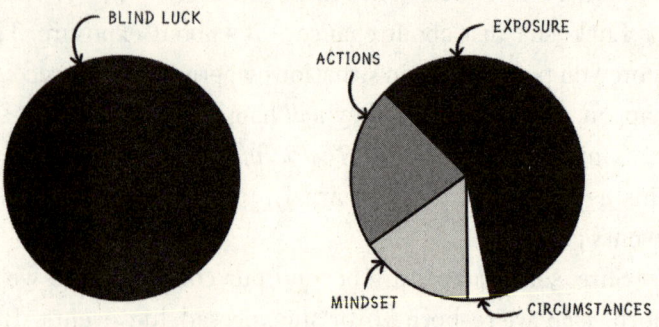

What it seems like   What it actually is

67

Tear Yourself Down or Build Yourself Up?

On the power of self-affirmation

You know that being assertive – asking for what you want – can be valuable for your personal and professional growth. But how often do you actually do it? How often do you ask for a promotion? A raise? An opportunity?

I know I've hesitated many times. I've stopped myself from sending a simple e-mail asking for help, convincing myself the other person was too busy to be interested. But deep down, I wasn't just worried about their response – I was protecting myself from possible rejection.

One of the most common fears we all experience is the fear of rejection. It stops us from going after what we want and keeps us playing small.

You don't ask for the opportunity that you want. You don't put yourself forward for the promotion that you know you deserve or the raise that you desire. You don't voice your ideas in that important meeting.

Why? Because rejection stings. It makes us question our self-worth.

But here's the thing: The worst kind of rejection is self-rejection.

If rejection from others is painful, rejecting yourself before even trying is far worse. So, how do we counteract this fear? By strengthening our self-belief.

Psychologist Claude Steele's *self-affirmation theory* suggests that when we affirm our core values – what truly matters to us – we reinforce our self-worth. This makes us more resilient and better equipped to handle challenges.

Amy Cuddy, in her book *Presence*, shares how taking time to affirm yourself before entering a high-stakes situation can boost your confidence and sense of agency.

Try this simple but proven exercise: Before stepping into a situation where you might feel vulnerable – whether it's a big presentation, a difficult conversation or an important request – take a few minutes to affirm your values.

Here's how:

1. **Identify one of your core values.** Something deeply important to you like integrity, kindness, courage, mindfulness.
2. **Reflect on a time you lived that value.** Write about a moment when you embodied it.
3. **Remind yourself that this value defines you, not external outcomes.**

For example, if your core value is perseverance, remind yourself: I've faced challenges before and found a way through. No matter the outcome, I will show up fully.

A basic need that we all have is to maintain a positive self-identity. When you proactively affirm your values and beliefs, you increase your sense of personal power. Not only do you then feel more confident in asking for what you want, you also increase your capacity to handle rejection. What's fascinating is that this works even if the value you are affirming has no direct connection to the situation at hand.

Here's my challenge for you: Think of one word that describes you at your best. Set a timer for ten minutes and write about a time when you recently demonstrated this quality. Now use this heightened sense of personal power to ask for something you want today, however small.

Because when you believe in yourself first, the world starts to believe in you too.

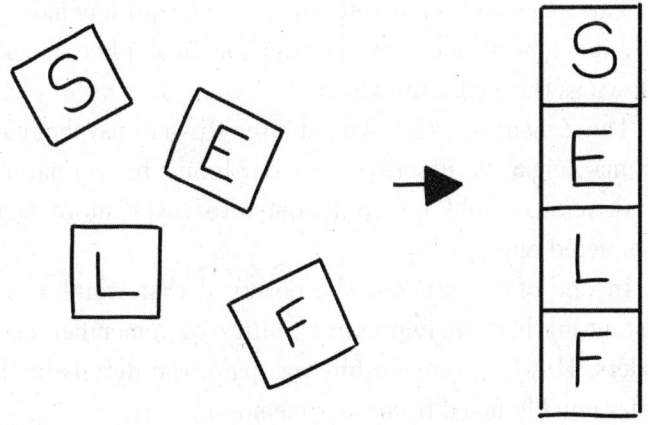

68

Open Loops or Closed Loops?
On freeing your presence of mind

You've wrapped up your work for the day and are looking forward to unwinding. But as you sit with loved ones or try to relax, your mind keeps pulling you back – unfinished emails, unresolved tasks, decisions left hanging.

Even if you're no longer at your desk, your brain hasn't quite left work behind.

This lingering mental tension isn't just a quirk of modern life, it's a well-documented psychological phenomenon known as the Zeigarnik effect.

The Zeigarnik effect, named after Russian psychologist Bluma Zeigarnik, describes how our brains have a natural tendency to hold on to incomplete tasks more than completed ones.

In one of her studies, she observed that waiters in a restaurant had an impressive ability to remember open orders. However, once a bill was paid, the details of the order quickly faded from their memory.

This study revealed something powerful: Your brain is wired to hold on to unfinished business.

This is why, after a long workday, you might struggle to be fully present at home. If you leave tasks unfinished, your brain keeps them top of mind, creating stress and mental clutter.

As a mindfulness practitioner, I am always thinking about what habits I can adopt to help my mind be more present. A lot of people recommend building a mindful morning routine to begin your day with the right frame of mind. While that can work wonders, I've found there's another routine that is even more powerful – a mindful evening routine.

How we end the day is just as important – if not more important – as how we begin the day. Chances are the emotions you end the day with will carry over into the morning. If you want to set the right tone for your day, get a head start the night before.

How can you make sure you don't let the Zeigarnik effect take away your peace of mind? There are two simple but effective strategies you can adopt:

One, prioritize meaningful tasks early. Identify your most important tasks for the day and tackle them first. Even if minor tasks remain unfinished, completing the key ones will give you a sense of accomplishment and closure.

Two, create a shutdown ritual. Put a strategy in place for closing all open mental loops. Look at your task list and take stock of what you did and didn't do. For each item that is still incomplete, create a mini plan for how and when you might tackle it the following day. This is equivalent to closing that open mental loop.

And then, if you *really* want to give your brain a powerful signal that you are done with the workday and ready to switch off, do what productivity expert Cal Newport does. At the end of your task list, in big bold letters, write the words or say out loud: Done or Shutdown Complete!

This simple practice tells your brain that it doesn't need to keep thinking about unfinished work because you've already planned when and how you'll tackle it.

As Newport says, 'When you work, work hard. When you're done, be done.'

Your ability to be fully present and at peace depends on how well you close open loops at the end of the day.

So, what's one simple shutdown ritual you can create to give your mind the closure it needs?

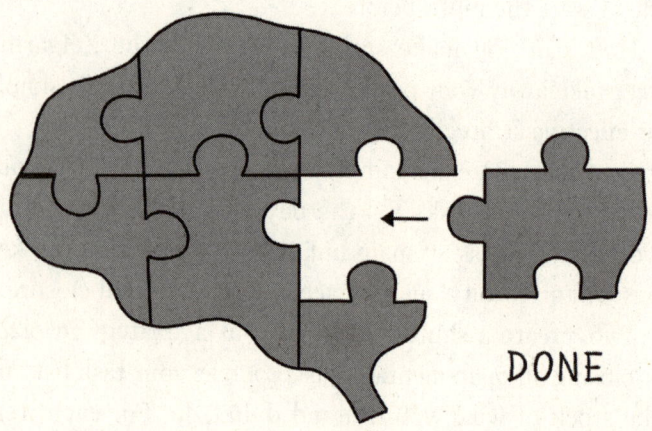

69

Have To or Get To?

On transforming obligation into gratitude

It's easy to feel overwhelmed by the endless to-do lists that fill our days. You want to excel at work, you want to make sure everything at home is well taken care of, all while pursuing a number of personal goals, including taking care of your health and fitness.

How do you find the motivation – and the energy – to do all the things that are important? Especially since, let's be honest, you may not always look forward to doing many of them.

What if a simple shift in perspective could change how we approach our daily tasks?

Instead of saying, 'I have to', try saying, 'I get to.'

This small change in language can have a profound impact on how we perceive our responsibilities. Consider these everyday examples:

Instead of 'I have to do my taxes,' say 'I *get to* do my taxes,' which acts as a subtle reminder of how fortunate you are to be earning an income that allows you to pay taxes.

Instead of saying 'I have to go to the gym today,' say

'I *get to* go to the gym today,' which reminds you of how lucky you are to have the time, space and resources to be able to focus on your health.

Instead of saying 'I have to help my child with homework,' say 'I *get to* help my child with homework.' For me, this is a reminder of how precious this phase of my son's life is. I know there will soon be a time when he won't need my help as much and I will miss feeling as needed as I do today.

This simple reframing shifts tasks from being burdens to opportunities – opportunities to contribute, to grow and to appreciate what we have.

Psychologists have long studied the connection between mindset and motivation. Research shows that when we view an activity as a privilege rather than an obligation, we're more likely to engage with it enthusiastically and consistently. Gratitude, in particular, has been shown to increase overall happiness, reduce stress and burnout and improve resilience and well-being.

By reframing our daily tasks as things we *get* to do, we cultivate a mindset of appreciation rather than resentment. The more you practise this, the more you'll realize that even the most mundane responsibilities hold meaning.

The question I have for you is: 'What is one thing that you *get to* do today?'

Have To or Get To?

70

Past or Future?
On what shapes you more

How you think about your past and your future shapes you in profound ways. Question is which one of the two – your past or your future – has a bigger influence on how you show up in the present?

Let me elaborate. Look at your actions and behaviors in the present moment. Now reflect on the following questions: Why are you choosing to spend this day the way that you are? Why are you prioritizing certain goals over others? Why did you choose to pick up and read this book?

Are these actions a function of your past – of the experiences you've had in life? Or are they a function of your future – the hopes, goals and dreams you have for the path ahead?

Traditional psychology, influenced by thinkers like Freud and Jung, suggests that we are largely shaped by our past. Our childhood experiences, past traumas and ingrained habits dictate how we show up in the world. But modern research suggests otherwise – our future and the way we imagine it may have a far greater influence than we realize.

Dr Benjamin Hardy in his book *Be Your Future Self Now* argues that those who focus more on their future than their past tend to be more resilient, adaptive and successful. Studies of war survivors, including Holocaust survivors, reveal a common theme – those who held onto a vision of a better future were more likely to survive and thrive.

Victor Frankl, a psychiatrist and Holocaust survivor, who lost his family in a concentration camp and went on to write about his experience in the bestseller *Man's Search for Meaning*, says this: 'In the Nazi concentration camps, one could have witnessed that those who knew that there was a task waiting for them to fulfill were most apt to survive.' Quoting Nietzsche he added, 'He who has a why to live for can bear almost any how.'

This idea is further supported by a concept in positive psychology introduced by Martin Seligman called 'prospection'. Seligman – considered the father of positive psychology – says what sets humans apart from other living beings is our ability to prospect – to imagine new possibilities and alternate futures for ourselves and work towards them. While animals rely on instincts and past conditioning, humans can visualize alternative futures and take actions to bring them to life.

If the future holds such power over our present, how can we use it to shape our decisions?

First, get clear on your future self. Imagine yourself five years from now. What do you want to be doing? Who do you want to become? The clearer this vision, the more influence it has over your present actions.

Second, set big, meaningful goals. As business coach

Dan Sullivan says, *'The only way to make your present better is to make your future bigger.'* Having a compelling future goal pulls you forward and keeps you from being stuck in past limitations.

Third, make decisions based on where you're going, not where you've been. Before making a big decision, ask yourself: 'Is this choice leading me toward the future I want or is it keeping me in my past?'

No matter what has happened in your past, your future is still unwritten. **So what will shape your next move?** Will it be the weight of the past or the promise of the future?

71

A Downward Spiral or an Upward Spiral?

On how your mindset shapes your reality

You're scrolling through social media when you see a competitor featured on a prestigious '40-under-40' list. Or a colleague showing off her six-pack abs. Or a friend jetting off on a dreamy vacation, radiating pure joy.

What do you feel in that moment?

If you're like most people, you might experience a twinge of jealousy. Or worse, a sinking feeling as you think, 'Why don't I have that? What am I doing wrong?'

Comparison is deeply wired into our psychology. In fact, a recent study by Amy Summerville of Miami University found that as much as 10 per cent of our thoughts involve comparisons of some kind. From an evolutionary standpoint, evaluating where we stood within our social group was key to survival. But in today's hyper-connected world, it can be overwhelming, leading us into a downward spiral of negativity.

The good news? While the instinct to compare may be automatic, how we respond to those comparisons is a choice. You don't have to eliminate comparison – you just need to reframe it. Instead of letting it drain you, you can use it as a tool to lift yourself up.

The next time you catch yourself comparing, try this – silently wish the other person well. You might say something like:

I wish you well.

I wish you success.

I wish you even greater joy.

At first this might feel counterintuitive. But research suggests it can be a game-changer.

Dr Barbara Fredrickson, a leading expert in positive psychology, has spent over two decades studying the impact of positive emotions. She found that cultivating feelings like appreciation and gratitude literally broadens our thinking. It allows us to generate more ideas, recognize more opportunities and take inspired action.

In one study, participants who intentionally practiced positive emotions were significantly more likely to use phrases like 'I can' and 'I would like to', indicating they felt more empowered and resourceful. Fredrickson calls this the Broaden-and-Build Theory – the idea that positive emotions don't just feel good in the moment – they actively build our resilience, creativity and ability to solve problems.

So why does wishing someone well work?

Because it shifts you from a mindset of scarcity to one of abundance. It reminds you that there's more than enough success, joy and fulfillment to go around. It also helps you break free from the comparison trap and refocus on your own path.

When you embrace a mindset of appreciation instead of competition, your brain starts asking better questions. What can I learn from this person's success? How can I apply their strategies to my own goals? What unique strengths do I have that I can build upon?

Over time, you'll find that comparison doesn't have to be a source of stress. Instead, it can become a source of motivation, helping you refine your vision and take action toward your own dreams.

Comparison can either hold you back or propel you forward. It can trap you in self-doubt or it can be a catalyst for growth. The key is to be intentional about which spiral you feed – negativity or positivity. The choice is yours.

Just like a water lily blooms when it soaks in sunlight, your mind expands when you feed it with gratitude, joy and compassion.

So here's my question for you: Who is someone you can celebrate today, even if by silently wishing them well? And what action – big or small – do you feel inspired to take toward your own goals?

72

Avoid Being Wrong or Find Joy In It?

On the power of a growth mindset

The other day I was having a conversation with a friend when I casually said, 'Oh, that sounds like the blind leading the blind.'

My friend looked visibly uncomfortable before gently pointing out that phrases like 'blind', 'tone-deaf' or 'lame' are considered offensive to people with disabilities. I was deeply embarrassed. I hadn't considered that perspective before.

Let me ask you – how do you feel when you realize you're wrong about something? Most of us feel defensive or even ashamed. We instinctively tie our identity and self-worth to being right, so when a belief of ours is challenged, it feels like a threat.

But here's the thing: if we resist being wrong, we also resist learning. If we want to grow, we have to reframe our relationship with mistakes.

It all comes down to becoming conscious of what we are attaching our identity to. As organizational psychologist Adam Grant explains in *Think Again*, true personal growth happens when we detach our identity from our opinions and root it instead in our values.

Instead of defining yourself as someone who is always right, what if you defined yourself as someone who lives by core values like courage, humility and kindness, above all else? Then the next time an idea you hold comes into question, you can say:

'Yes I was wrong, but I had the humility to admit it.'

'Yes I was wrong, but I had the courage to have a difficult conversation about it.'

'Yes I was wrong, but I chose kindness towards others and myself in that moment.'

When you shift your mindset in this way, being wrong is no longer a blow to your ego. Instead, it becomes an opportunity to strengthen the values that truly matter to you.

In psychology, there's a term called *cognitive dissonance* – the discomfort we feel when our existing beliefs are challenged. But what if we saw that discomfort as a sign of growth?

Think about the times in your life when you changed your mind about something important. Maybe you once held a rigid belief but later expanded your perspective. Maybe you thought you had all the answers, only to discover an entirely new way of thinking.

Each of these moments made you wiser. Each mistake, each correction, helped shape the person you are today.

Avoid Being Wrong or Find Joy In It?

The most open-minded, intelligent people are not the ones who are never wrong, they are the ones who are *willing* to be wrong.

They don't fear making mistakes because they know mistakes are just stepping stones toward deeper understanding. They embrace feedback, seek out diverse viewpoints and challenge their own assumptions.

Here's my question for you: Can you think of a time when you changed your mind about something important? How did that shift help you grow?

Could be the opportunity to

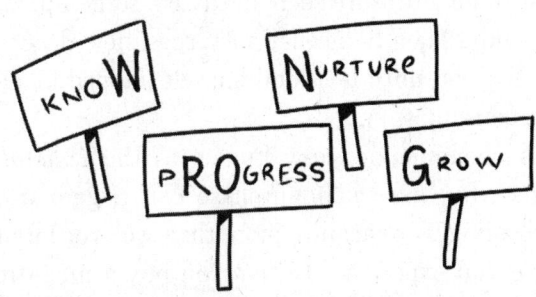

73

Less or More?

On the Diderot Effect and conscious consumption

Denis Diderot, the French philosopher behind one of the first encyclopaedias, spent most of his life in poverty. That is until Catherine the Great of Russia bought his encyclopaedia collection, suddenly making him a wealthy man.

What did Diderot do with his newfound wealth? He bought himself a luxurious new robe.

And that's where it all began.

Once he had the robe, his old chair looked shabby in comparison, so he bought a new one. The new chair made the rest of his furniture seem outdated, so he upgraded his entire study. Then he needed new rugs, new decor and on and on it went, until he found himself trapped in a cycle of endless consumption.

This phenomenon, now known as the *Diderot Effect*, explains why one small purchase can trigger a domino effect, leading us to acquire more than we ever intended.

Have you experienced this? You buy a nice dress and now you need nice shoes or a bag to match. You move into a larger house and now you need more stuff to put inside it.

We live in an age of abundance. There are more career paths, lifestyle options, entertainment choices and consumer goods than ever before. Logically, you'd think this would make us happier. But as research shows, this often has the opposite effect.

For one, more choices lead to decision fatigue – the more options we have, the harder it is to decide. Two, even if you make a choice, you experience some amount of dissatisfaction as you wonder if you made the *best* choice. Barry Schwartz calls this the Paradox of Choice – having more options doesn't make us more content – it often makes us more anxious.

Could there be a better way?

I am learning to cultivate what I like to call the 'Reverse Diderot Effect'.

Years ago, frustrated by mindless consumption, I made a radical decision. I stopped shopping for clothes entirely. What started as a short-term challenge turned into five years of not buying a single new outfit. It was difficult at first but over time it became a core part of my identity and I started to take great pride in living consciously.

Instead of accumulating more, I began *upcycling* by revamping old sarees into new outfits. Almost every speaking engagement I've had in the last five years, I've done in an upcycled piece of clothing.

And you know what? I've never felt freer.

With fewer clothes I had less need for accessories to go with my clothes. With less time spent on shopping, I had more time for other activities like reading. With fewer resources spent on clothes, I could invest in things with more lasting value to power my own learning and development.

With less mental bandwidth used for deciding what to wear every day, I could focus on more important decisions such as how to expand my business to serve more women.

Here are three ways in which you can overcome the Diderot Effect and reclaim your mental and emotional space. One, start with small, self-imposed limits – try going just one month without shopping. Two, eliminate triggers – unfollow people or accounts that encourage mindless consumption. Three, adopt a 'buy one, give one' strategy – whenever you buy something new, aim to give something away, especially to those who need it.

The most precious piece of real estate you have is your mind. The fewer distractions you allow in, the more space you create for clarity, purpose and joy.

My question for you: Where in your life can you reverse the Diderot Effect?

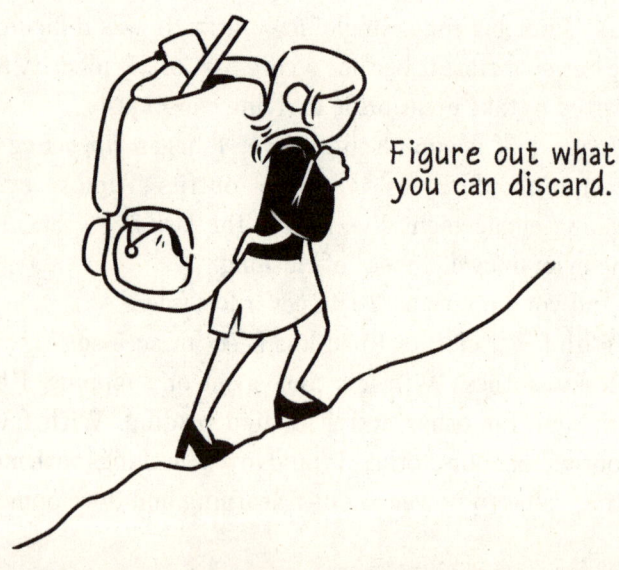
Figure out what you can discard.

74

Fact or Story?

On reframing your thoughts for clarity

I was sitting at a coffee shop recently when I spotted someone I hadn't seen in a while. I was quite pleased to see her. When she looked in my direction, I excitedly smiled and waved at her. But she didn't wave back. In fact, she walked right past me.

Immediately my mind started spinning: *Did I do something to upset her? Maybe she doesn't like me anymore. Maybe I should have kept in touch more.* I must have spent the next several minutes caught in this loop, trying to figure out *why* she had ignored me.

Have you had something similar happen to you? As you try to make sense of a situation, your thoughts weave a story – one that doesn't serve you well.

We do this all the time.

You send an email and don't get a response. Your mind jumps to: *They must think my request isn't important.*

You present an idea in a meeting and someone looks distracted. Your mind whispers: *They must find my ideas boring.*

You invite a friend out and they cancel last minute. The story you tell yourself? *They don't value our friendship as much as I do.*

Our minds are story-making machines. We are conditioned to create a story, any story, just to make sense of the world. But in the absence of actual information about what the truth really is, it doesn't help to be spinning these stories. Often these stories – while compelling – aren't true.

So how do we stop ourselves from going down a rabbit hole of blame or shame in these situations? Dr Amishi Jha, author of *Peak Mind*, offers two powerful questions to break this cycle.

1. **What do I know for sure?** Strip away all assumptions and stick only to the verifiable facts.
2. **What is the story I am telling myself?** Acknowledge that your interpretation is just one of many possibilities.

When I applied these questions to my coffee shop experience, here's what I knew for sure: I saw someone I knew. She appeared to look in my direction. I waved. She did not appear to wave back. That was it. Everything else – my assumptions, my interpretations – was a story I had created.

Also, I realized there were countless reasons she may not have acknowledged me. Maybe she didn't actually see me. Maybe she was lost in thought. Maybe she was having a bad day.

As soon as I dropped the story I had created, I felt calmer.

Fact or Story?

This doesn't mean we ignore important signals. Sometimes we *do* need to get clarity. If your boss hasn't responded to an important email, instead of assuming the worst, you can follow up. If you're unsure how your idea landed in a meeting, you can ask for feedback.

But jumping to conclusions rarely serves us. The reality is that most people are too absorbed in their own worlds to be as focused on us as we think they are.

Here is an exercise I'd like to leave you with: At any point today, if you catch yourself overthinking a situation or interaction, I encourage you to consciously ask these two questions:

What do I know for sure?

What is a story I am telling myself?

It just might set you free.

75

The Pebble or the Bridge?
On finding meaning in small, daily actions

Think about something meaningful you're working toward right now. Maybe it's a big career goal, a personal dream or simply trying to show up as your best self each day. Have you ever felt like your day-to-day contributions were too small to matter? Like no matter how much effort you put in, at the end of the day, it still feels like a drop in the ocean?

If so, you're not alone. And perhaps this ancient story from Hindu mythology might shift your perspective – **of Lord Rama and the squirrel.**

Rama was preparing for war against the demon king Ravana. To reach Ravana's kingdom, Rama and his army needed to build a bridge across the ocean.

His army of monkeys worked tirelessly, carrying massive boulders to construct the bridge.

One day, they noticed a tiny squirrel scurrying back and forth, carrying small pebbles in its mouth and dropping them onto the bridge. The monkeys laughed. 'What difference will your tiny pebbles make?'

Curious, Rama approached the squirrel and asked, 'What are you doing?'

The squirrel replied, 'I am doing the best I can.'

Moved by its dedication, Rama gently stroked the squirrel's back, blessing it. To this day, Indian palm squirrels are said to have three stripes on their backs, believed to be Rama's fingerprints.

The lesson? Every small action matters.

Sometimes our tasks feel insignificant – you might want to quickly get through them to reach whatever end goal you are striving for. But each task you engage in, no matter how small or tedious, plays an important role in your journey of growth and evolution.

Take Tibetan Buddhist monks, for example. They spend weeks creating elaborate geometric patterns or *mandalas* out of coloured sand. Once the mandala is complete, it's left on display for some time, during which people can admire its beauty and contemplate its meaning.

But the most striking part of this practice is when it comes to an end. After the mandala has served its purpose, the monks gather in a ceremony to systematically dismantle it, sweeping the coloured sand back into a container.

Why do they do this? As my mentor Dr Srikumar Rao often says, 'It's not the end result that blesses you but the task itself, depending on the attitude that you bring to it.'

As you work toward your most cherished goals and dreams, you have a choice. You can remain focused on the final destination, hoping to find that pot of gold at the end of the rainbow. Or you can bring sincere appreciation and humility to every mundane task along the way – to every single pebble that you lift – knowing that each task is molding you into the person you will become. You are blessed not by the destination but by the journey itself.

My question to you: What's a goal you're working toward? Instead of fixating on the outcome, how can you bring more meaning and appreciation to the small steps along the way?

Because in the end, it's not just about building the bridge. It's about carrying the pebble.

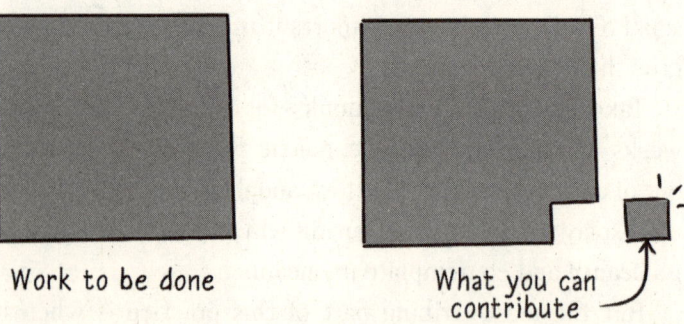

Work to be done   What you can contribute

76

Discomfort or Resentment?

On setting healthy boundaries for a balanced life

For as long as I can remember, I struggled to say no. I was a chronic people-pleaser, saying yes to almost everything – extra projects, last-minute favors, social commitments I had no energy for. I feared that if I said no, I would disappoint people or lose their affection.

It took me a long time to realize this truth: when you don't set boundaries, you don't just exhaust yourself. You also teach others to undervalue your time, energy and needs.

A boundary is a conscious decision about what you will and will not allow, whether physically, emotionally or mentally. It's about getting clear on where you draw the line. And for me, there were two fundamental shifts in belief that finally helped me set healthier boundaries.

The first was understanding that boundaries are not barriers. Many of us fear that setting boundaries will create distance in our relationships, that saying no will make us seem selfish or unkind. But the opposite is true. Boundaries are a form of self-respect and when you respect yourself, others learn to respect you too. Research even suggests that people who set clear boundaries tend to be more compassionate because they take responsibility for their own well-being instead of expecting others to do it for them.

The second realization was that I always had a choice: the temporary discomfort of saying no now or the long-term resentment of saying yes when I didn't mean it. Resentment lingers. Discomfort passes. As Brené Brown puts it, 'Choose discomfort over resentment.'

Once I understood the power of boundaries, I had to learn how to say no in a way that felt natural and compassionate. Here are five simple steps for saying no with kindness:

First, express gratitude. Thank the person who reached out for thinking of you for their request. This shows respect for the other person's needs and desires.

Second, provide a clear context for saying no. Honesty is key, but it's important to communicate in a way that's gentle and direct. For example, 'Thank you for thinking of me, but I don't have the bandwidth at the moment.' By providing a clear why for your no, it will feel softer and yet still have impact.

Third, depending on the context, offer a solution that still supports them. You might say, 'While I can't help you at the moment, here's something or someone who can be helpful.'

Fourth, express empathy. Recognize the impact your no may have. For example, 'I understand this may be disappointing and I wish I could help more.' This conveys care and empathy without over-explaining.

Finally, wish them well. End on a positive note: 'I wish you the best with this project. I hope it goes really well.' This leaves the conversation on a kind, supportive tone.

Whenever I feel guilt creeping in about saying no, I remind myself of this: *Every time I say no to something misaligned, I am saying yes to something that truly matters.*

Your time and energy are finite. The more you guard them, the more space you create for the work, relationships and experiences that bring you fulfillment.

So my question to you is: What is a healthy boundary that you'd like to set today?

Your boundaries will protect you

77

Contamination or Redemption?
On the stories we tell ourselves

Every day, we tell ourselves stories. Stories about who we are, what we've been through and what our experiences mean. These stories shape our identity – how we see ourselves and how we engage with the world.

Psychologist Dan McAdams, a pioneer in narrative psychology, discovered that the stories we tell about our lives tend to fall into two broad categories: redemption stories or contamination stories.

A redemption story is one where challenges, setbacks or pain lead to growth, meaning or positive transformation. For example, you might have lost a job, but that led you to discover a career you're truly passionate about. Or maybe a painful breakup helped you develop resilience and self-love. Or you grew up in poverty but that helped shape your values around hard work and humility. These stories turn struggle into strength.

A contamination story on the other hand is one where things start off well but take a turn for the worse and that's where the story gets stuck. A failed relationship, a lost opportunity, a mistake ... you tell yourself that things went downhill from there and never quite recovered.

McAdams suggests that redemptive narratives, characterized by growth and agency, imbue our lives with greater purpose and meaning. They reframe challenges as opportunities for personal development and setbacks as stepping stones toward a brighter future. Consider an individual who transforms childhood adversity into resilience or the caregiver who finds renewed purpose amidst tragedy. These narratives not only shape our understanding of ourselves but also drive us towards making a bigger contribution to society and future generations.

On the other hand, people who lean toward contamination stories are more likely to be anxious and depressed, as they struggle to make sense of their lives.

The reality is, no one's life is purely good or bad. It's the meaning you assign to your life that matters. In the story you tell yourself, you can either be the protagonist who overcomes adversities or simply succumbs to them.

The best part? You can rewrite your story at any time. If you've been telling yourself a contamination story, you don't have to stay stuck in it. You can reframe the past by asking: *What did I learn from this? How did this experience make me stronger? How did this challenge shape me into the person I am today?*

By reshaping our narratives, we can reshape our lives. You can edit, revise and reinterpret the stories you tell yourself and reclaim agency over your life. Even small edits like focusing on moments of gratitude or acts of kindness can lead to tangible shifts in behaviour, moving you towards a more purposeful existence. The choice between redemption and contamination is yours to make – let it be a conscious one.

My question to you: What story are you telling yourself? And how might you rewrite it to be a redemptive one?

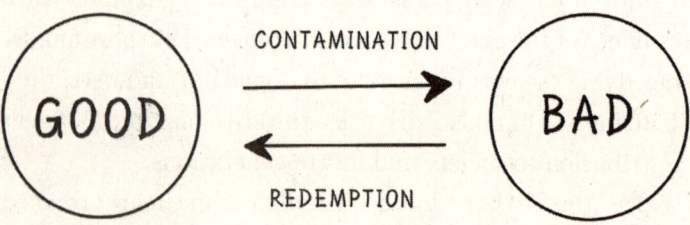

78

Decision or Sacrifice?
On reframing the choices you make

There are moments in life when we face difficult choices – leaving a stable job for something uncertain, prioritizing family over a career opportunity, choosing other obligations over self-care. In these moments we often say, 'I had to make a sacrifice.' But what if you didn't?

What if instead, you called it a decision?

It may seem like a small shift but the words we use to frame our experiences shape how we feel about them. Calling something a sacrifice implies loss, burden and an element of suffering. It suggests you are giving something up against your will. A decision on the other hand is an active, empowered choice – one that aligns with your values and priorities.

Carol Dweck's research on mindset tells us that how we frame our experiences significantly impacts our motivation and well-being. In her book *Mindset: The New Psychology of Success*, she explains that people with a fixed mindset see challenges as obstacles, whereas those with a growth mindset reframe difficulties as opportunities for learning and choice. If you tell yourself, 'I sacrificed my career for my family,' you might feel resentment. But if you say, 'I made a conscious decision to prioritize my family because that matters most to me,' you feel ownership and pride.

As Viktor Frankl wrote in *Man's Search for Meaning*, 'When we are no longer able to change a situation, we are challenged to change ourselves.'

Consider an Olympic athlete who wakes up at 4 a.m. every morning to train. If you asked them, 'Aren't you sacrificing sleep, social events and a "normal" life for this?' they would likely say, 'No, I'm choosing this because I want to be great.' The same applies to you. Are you sacrificing something or are you making a deliberate choice for something greater?

Psychologist Kelly McGonigal, in her book *The Upside of Stress*, explains that reframing an experience changes its emotional impact. When people view stress as something harmful, it takes a toll on their health and happiness. But when they see stress as a necessary part of growth, their resilience strengthens. The same principle applies to decisions. If you call it a sacrifice, it feels heavy. If you call it a decision, it becomes empowering.

So how can you apply this?

The next time you feel like you're making a sacrifice, pause and ask yourself:

1. What am I choosing instead?
2. How does this align with my values and long-term goals?
3. How does this decision reflect the life I want to create?

By making this shift, you reclaim your power. You stop seeing yourself as someone who *had* to give something up and instead as someone who *chose* to prioritize what truly matters.

Because life isn't about what you sacrifice – it's about what you choose.

My question to you: What decision are you making today that will serve your future self?

79

Good Thing or Bad Thing?

On letting go of judgement in uncertain times

'This is bad. Really bad. I joined this company because of her and she's gone!'

Ruchi, one of my coaching clients, was devastated. She had recently accepted a job, largely because she admired the hiring manager and was excited to work with her. But just a few weeks after Ruchi joined, her manager unexpectedly left the organization.

'This feels like a disaster,' she told me. 'I made the wrong choice.'

I listened, then asked, 'Have you heard the story of the farmer and the horse?'

'No, what's that about?'

There was once a man who managed a small farm with his son.

One day, their only horse ran away. The neighbours came to express their concern. 'Oh, that's too bad. How are you going to work the fields now?'

The farmer simply replied, 'Good thing, bad thing. Who knows?'

After a few days the horse returned, bringing another horse with it. Now, the neighbours exclaimed, 'Oh, how lucky! You can do twice as much work as before.' The farmer again replied, 'Good thing, bad thing. Who knows?'

The next day, the farmer's son fell off the new horse and broke his leg. The neighbours sighed, 'Now that he's incapacitated, he can't help you around. That's too bad.' And once again the farmer replied, 'Good thing, bad thing. Who knows?'

Soon, news came that a war had broken out. All young men were required to join the army and the fear was that many of them may not make it back. Because of his injury, the farmer's son was spared. The neighbours, now envious, said, 'How lucky! You get to keep your only son.'

The farmer smiled and said, 'Good thing, bad thing. Who knows?'

We are conditioned to label everything that happens to us as either good or bad. Instead, what if you were to hold back your judgment knowing that it's just part of the story you are telling yourself – that in fact, you don't know how this story will play out in the future?

While none of us can control what happens to us, we can control how we respond. When you put aside labels of good and bad, right and wrong, fair and unfair, you open yourself up to accepting the situation instead of fighting against it. Once you do that, you can decide your next best step with a clear mind.

As for Ruchi, she made a conscious choice to let go of her initial frustration and focus on making the most of her new role. She sought mentorship from other senior leaders, took ownership of key projects and leaned into her strengths. Before long, her work was recognized and she was promoted – to the same role as her former hiring manager.

Would that have happened if her manager had stayed? Probably not.

This is why I always return to the same mantra: Good thing, bad thing. Who knows?

My question to you: What event in your life – past or present – are you attaching a label to? What might open up for you if you let go of that label?

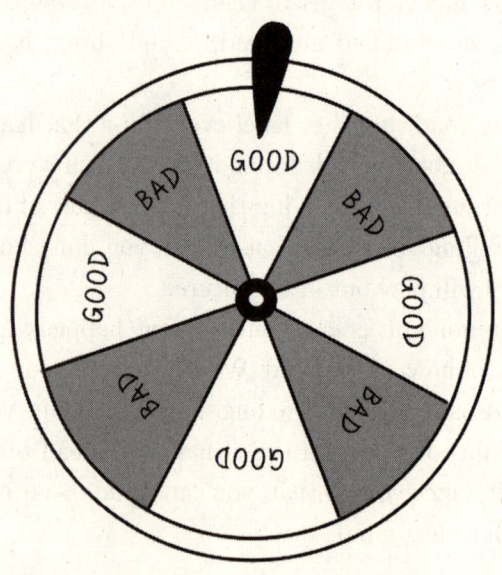

80

Here or There?

On breaking free from destination addiction

A few months ago, I went on a long-awaited girls' trip to Vietnam.

I had every intention of relaxing and soaking in the experience. But even as we explored breathtaking landscapes and indulged in local cuisine, I found myself mentally racing ahead. I was always wondering, *'What's next?'*

One morning, we set off to visit Ninh Binh, a stunning region known for its limestone cliffs and ancient temples. To reach one of the most famous temples, we had to climb 500 steep steps.

'How long does it typically take?' I asked our tour guide.

'About twenty minutes,' he replied.

'Great,' I thought, 'I'll do it in fifteen.'

With that, I took off, determined to reach the top as quickly as possible. But after just a hundred steps, drenched in sweat and gasping for breath, I had no choice but to stop. As I looked up, I saw something I hadn't noticed before

– an incredible panoramic view of lush green valleys and winding rivers.

And in that moment, a few thoughts hit me like lightning bolts.

Why am I rushing? Where am I running to?

Even if I reached the summit in record time, so what? What was I trying to prove? And to whom?

Maybe you've had a similar experience. You push yourself to achieve more, to hit the next milestone, to get to the next level – only to find that when you do, the happiness you feel is fleeting.

This is called 'destination addiction' – the belief that happiness is always just around the corner. The reason why we do this is often a deep-seated sense of inadequacy – feeling like you are not enough. You feel you have to constantly prove yourself to others and your own self and that your achievements will help compensate for that inadequacy. You tell yourself:

I'll feel worthy when I get that promotion.
I'll feel worthy when I hit my ideal weight.
I'll feel worthy when I finally take that dream vacation.

But the problem is, once we reach one goal, another one quickly takes its place. The chase never ends. Psychologists call this the 'hedonic treadmill' – our tendency to return to a baseline level of happiness no matter what we achieve.

If we are always running from one peak experience to another – one goal to another – our existence starts to feel purely functional. It's as if we're going down a checklist, checking off achievements. But when our self-worth is tied so strongly to achievement, we inevitably experience a restlessness until we reach the next destination – the next achievement – to enjoy a temporary respite from not feeling enough.

How do we break free from this endless cycle? There are two things that are helping me.

One, spend more time doing activities that bring you joy and that have nothing to do with achievement. Take a walk in nature. Dance in your living room. Sit in silence with a cup of tea. Appreciate art in a museum. These moments remind us that life isn't just about checking off goals, it's about experiencing them.

Two, shift your focus from personal achievement to the positive impact you have or hope to have on others. Instead of measuring life by what you achieve, measure it by how much you contribute. This perspective shift can be incredibly empowering. Rather than focusing on your perceived weaknesses and inadequacies, you begin to appreciate the inherent value and power you have to make a difference. When you do, the pressure to constantly 'arrive' disappears.

Back in Ninh Binh, when I finally reached the top, the view was indeed spectacular. But here's what struck me: we only had ten minutes at the summit before we had to start the descent. We spent twice as much time climbing as we did enjoying the destination.

That's when I realized that if most of our time is spent in the climb, why not learn to love it?

As Robert Holden once said: 'Beware of destination addiction ... until you give up on the idea that happiness is somewhere else, it will never be where you are.'

My question to you: What's one thing you can do today *not* as an achievement but purely for the joy of the experience?

Look forward but also focus on the now.

81

The Easy Life or a Life of Growth?
On the choices that define us

Every day we are faced with endless choices. The average person reportedly makes 33,000 to 35,000 decisions daily.

Some of our choices are mundane: What do I eat? What do I wear? What task do I check off first from my to-do list? Others are more profound: How do I treat others? What values do I hold in high regard? How do I spend each day in a way that leaves me feeling joy and fulfilment?

These daily choices, big and small, ultimately shape the person that you become, the life you build and the happiness and success that you experience.

Legend has it that at one point in his journey, the mythical hero Hercules found himself at a crossroads. Uncertain what path to take in life, he was confronted by two goddesses.

The first goddess pushed ahead and told Hercules that her friends called her Eudaimonia or happiness. She promised a life of pure pleasure and luxury with little to no effort – if he chose to follow her, he would have it all. What she didn't reveal was that her real name was Kakia or vice.

The other goddess listened calmly before stepping forward and told Hercules that if he chose to follow her, his life would be extraordinarily challenging and demand the best from him. But his noble deeds would win him the favour of the gods and the respect of his people.

This goddess was called Arete, the Greek word for excellence or virtue.

Each of us faces a similar choice daily. You can either pick the easy life – and the allure of the easy life filled with pleasures is indeed strong and hard to resist. *Or* you can embrace life's challenges and use the power of your virtues and values to face these challenges with wisdom, courage and compassion.

The decision is yours to make. Hercules, of course, chose the path of virtue. What about you?

According to Harvard Business School professor Gerald Zaltman, 95 per cent of the mental processes behind our decisions take place in the subconscious mind. This is by evolutionary design – it would be too overwhelming for the brain to weigh more than 30,000 choices one by one. Despite this, how can we ensure that we are able to make our most important choices consciously?

Here is one tool I can offer you that will help you make better choices intentionally: journaling, especially in the morning.

You could engage in free-writing, what Julia Cameron of *The Artist's Way* calls 'morning pages'. Each morning, fill at least three pages with an unfiltered stream of thought.

Alternatively, you could give yourself a set of questions to respond to. How would I like to show up today? What will make this day a good one? What am I committing to today?

This simple process will help you make more balanced decisions. When you write by hand, both the left and right sides of your brain team up. While your logical side helps grasp your emotions, your creative side allows you to think outside the box. Jointly, they empower you to process complex decisions, find clarity and feel more confident about the choices you make. Most importantly, writing helps you get off 'autopilot' mode and live your life a lot more consciously.

The easy path is tempting. It's comfortable, familiar and risk-free. But the question is: What kind of life do you want to build?

Do you want a life that is easy or one that is meaningful?

Choosing growth doesn't mean rejecting joy or pleasure. It means knowing when to push yourself beyond the immediate reward and embrace challenges that shape you into the person you aspire to be.

Hercules made his choice. What will yours be?

A question for you to journal on today: What are the choices you would like to make today that will leave you feeling proud?

The Conscious Choice

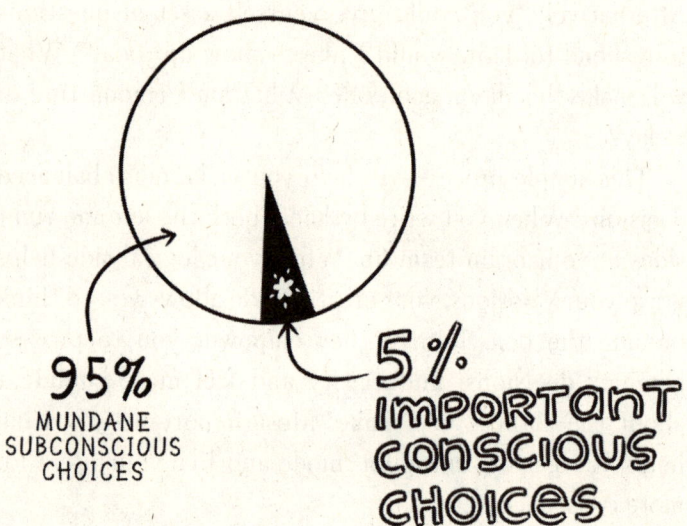

82

Ahead or Behind?

On running your own race

At some point, we've all had that creeping feeling: *I should be further along by now.* Maybe you've compared yourself to a colleague who's getting promoted faster, a friend who seems to have their life figured out or a peer who's already built a thriving business.

In these moments, it's easy to think you're falling behind, as if life is some kind of race.

Psychologist Daniel Kahneman found that our brains are wired for relative thinking. We measure our success not by objective milestones, but by how we compare to those around us.

That's why someone earning $100,000 in a community where everyone earns $50,000 feels successful, while someone earning the same amount in a community where everyone makes $200,000 feels like a failure. It's not about where you are, it's about who you're measuring yourself against.

The problem with feeling like you're behind is that you're often comparing yourself to someone playing a completely different game.

I want you to try the following experiment:

Imagine you were to ask a hundred people you know what their starting point was in life. How many different answers do you think you would get? A hundred.

Some people you know were probably goal-oriented from the get-go. Others found their drive later in life. Some people were born with a silver spoon in their mouth, with all the necessary resources to take advantage of key opportunities. Others struggled, relying on hard work and their sheer will and determination.

Now imagine you were to ask those same hundred people what the end point of their careers might be. What is their ultimate goal – the point at which they would feel they had arrived at their chosen destination? Again, chances are you would get a hundred different answers.

Some people want to retire by forty. Some want to keep going till they hit a certain milestone in their career, whether that's a financial goal ('I want to become a millionaire') or an impact goal ('I want to change a million lives'). Meanwhile there are some who may never want to stop working. In other words, they have no end point.

Finally, imagine going back to those same hundred people to ask them how they measure their success. Once again, you would get a hundred varied answers.

Some might measure success by the amount of acclaim they garner, or the wealth they accumulate. Some may be focused on the number of lives they positively touch, while for others, success may just be a function of how happy and successful their kids are.

Here's the point of this thought experiment. In any game, to determine winners and losers, you need three things.

Ahead or Behind?

One, a common starting point.

Two, a common end point.

Three, a common set of rules by which to measure and compare performance.

In life, you will rarely find a situation where all three conditions are met. When everyone around you has a different starting point, a different end point and their own measure of success, how can you judge who is 'behind' and who is 'ahead'?

Here's the truth: There is no universal race. You are running your race, and I am running mine.

Instead of asking, *Am I ahead or behind?* ask: *Am I moving toward what truly matters to me? Am I growing into the person I want to become? Am I making choices that align with my values, not someone else's expectations?*

As Naval Ravikant put it, 'Life is a single-player game.'

You get to choose which game you are going to play. You get to choose how long you will play it. And only you get to choose how you will measure your success.

My question to you: What game are you playing and how are you choosing to measure your success?

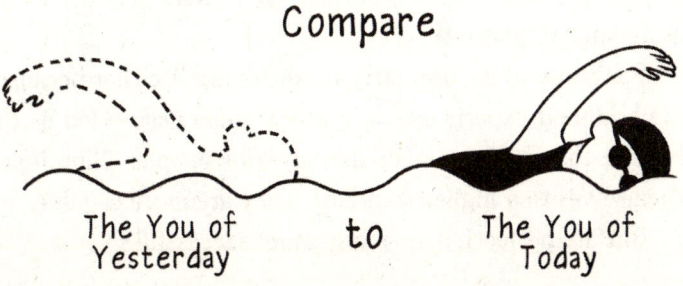

83

Quantity or Quality?

On the path to mastery

Nietzsche famously wrote, 'What doesn't kill you will make you stronger.' This axiom has been repeated so many times that many of us don't even question it. We have accepted it as a holy truth.

Except Nietzsche was wrong. Let's look at one big area where this may *not* be true.

Perfectionism.

Perfectionism has become something of a hidden epidemic. I see scores of my coaching clients, both women and men, suffering from it. I myself am a recovering perfectionist and not yet free from its clutches.

The question is, why do so many of us wear perfectionism as a badge of honour?

For many of us, our early conditioning – either because of childhood experiences or cultural influences – led us to believe that perfectionists are superior people. They hold themselves to a higher standard. They are more capable.

But are perfectionists really more successful?

Quantity or Quality?

The answer, as leading expert Thomas Curran shares in *The Perfection Trap*, is a big fat NO!

Here are two reasons why:

One, perfectionists may work longer and harder on a task than needed, which leads to burnout and compromises their health. That, in turn, gets in the way of creating superior results.

Two, their intense focus on perfect outcomes creates a lot of anxiety, which leads perfectionists to procrastinate more than non-perfectionists. That means, at the end of the day, they are putting out less work, learning less than others and therefore growing less than others.

And that is why Nietzsche's words cannot be taken at face value. Perfectionists are killing themselves to attain their impossibly high standards and it is creating both greater burnout and anxiety, neither of which are making them stronger or more successful.

How do we get over this crippling tendency? A fascinating story shared by David Bayles and Ted Orland in their book *Art and Fear* may provide an answer.

A ceramics teacher announced on the first day of class that he was dividing the students into two groups. Group one would be graded solely on the *quantity* of work, while group two would be judged on the *quality* of what they produced. When grading time arrived, the teacher observed something fascinating: the works of the highest quality were all produced by the group being graded for quantity.

By churning out pot after pot, they improved with each attempt. Meanwhile, the quality group spent too much time theorizing about perfection, producing far less and learning far less in the process.

The moral of the story: if high quality of work is what you are ultimately striving for, focus on quantity rather than perfection. Create as many imperfect pots as you can and learn from each one.

If you are trying to make your voice heard at your organization, know that the first few times you present, it will be imperfect. You voice will shake and you will feel anxious. Keep raising your hand for one speaking opportunity after another anyway.

If you are trying to build a bigger network, know that your first few attempts at connecting with senior leaders will feel awkward. You may not have your elevator pitch perfectly nailed and that's okay. Keep trying and keep reaching out to people anyway.

If you are trying to build a stronger presence online, know that your first few posts on LinkedIn may not get good engagement and that's alright. Keep learning from each post and keep writing anyway.

Over time, each imperfect pot that you put out in the world will teach you something about what to do more of and what to do less of. Each learning will imbue you with greater confidence and help you produce better results over time.

Mastery is not about being perfect. It's about staying in motion.

Here's my question to you: What's one thing you've been overthinking or delaying because you want it to be perfect? Instead, what imperfect action can you take today?

Quantity or Quality?

THIS   comes from   THIS

84

Autotelic or Exotelic?

On finding joy in the process

Vincent Van Gogh is widely considered to be one of the greatest painters of all time. He started his career rather late, relatively speaking. He didn't pick up a pencil to sketch seriously until he was twenty-seven.

He knew little about anatomy or perspective – two essential skills for artists of the time. His first few attempts were not promising, to say the least. By age thirty, he was living in poverty. But he was still sketching, though mostly for an audience of two – his brother and sister-in-law.

In time, he discovered colours and the rest, as they say, is history.

He started churning out painting after painting after painting. It didn't take long for him to become one of the most prolific painters of all time, producing 700 drawings and 800 oil paintings, all within a span of ten years.

Now for the truly startling fact, do you know how many paintings he sold while he was alive?

One. That's right. Only one.

His work, considered unorthodox at the time, was largely rejected by society. He only gained fame posthumously.

Vincent Van Gogh was what renowned psychologist Mihaly Csikszentmihalyi would call an 'autotelic' person.

Autotelic is a combination of two Greek words: *auto*, which means self and *telic*, which means goal. An autotelic activity, in other words, is 'a self-contained activity that is not done with the expectation of future benefit but simply because the doing itself is the reward.' Similarly an autotelic personality, as Csikszentmihalyi writes in *Flow*, pays attention to an activity for its own sake, not for any external reward.

For instance, if you choose to play poker purely for the love of the game, that experience would be autotelic for you. On the other hand, if you play it for money or to gain a competitive ranking, then it would be an 'exotelic' experience – motivated by an outside goal.

When you approach your goals with an autotelic mindset, you don't ask:

Will I succeed?

Will people approve?

Will they like this?

What will that say about me?

Instead, you pursue the activity simply because it brings you joy. It enables you to learn and grow. And maybe, just maybe, it also helps or inspires others.

I decided to write about this idea – and indeed, all the ideas in this book – not knowing how many people will read it or like it. I chose to do so because it gives me great joy to write about ideas that inspire me.

Few people are fully autotelic. There are many times when we have to do things out of necessity or a sense of duty. That said, there are people who choose to give their full attention to tasks, even the mundane ones, because they find inherent value in doing so. They don't attend to a task because it is interesting. Rather, the task *becomes* interesting because they have consciously chosen to give their attention to it.

You can live an exotelic life – to do things because you have to, because they look good or because they lead to external success.

Or, you can choose an autotelic life – do things because they light you up, because they make you grow, because they bring you joy.

My question to you: What's something you love doing for its own sake? How can you bring more of that into your life?

EXOTELIC   vs.   AUTOTELIC

85

Quit or Persevere?

On knowing when to walk away

About a decade ago, I hit a point in my life where the cost of continuing down the path I was on felt higher than any alternative. I'd just graduated with an MBA from NYU Stern and was earning a six-figure income at a reputable investment firm in New York. I should have been thrilled, right?

Wrong.

There was a quiet voice inside me that kept saying, 'Bhavna, this isn't your path. This isn't it. This isn't it!'

'Shhhhhh,' I would say to that voice. 'Do you not know I just spent over $120,000 on an MBA? I have a great job. I'm living the life. I'm now a US citizen. What do you want from me?'

'You have to find your unique way of making a bigger impact in the world!' the voice would fight back. And it kept getting louder and louder, to the point where it was no longer a whisper but a piercing scream that I couldn't ignore.

And so, I quit.

I quit my corporate career to find my own path. I quit a belief system that my worth could only be measured by the external metrics of success that I'd become conditioned to seek. I quit a life of comfort and ease and traded it for one of meaningful struggle as an entrepreneur.

Over the years, I have quit many other things that no longer served me – some for short periods of time, some forever. I once quit eating sugar for a hundred days. I quit shopping for five years. And I am doing my best to quit complaining forever.

We've been told that winners never quit and quitters never win. But what if that's not true?

Many of us hold onto jobs, relationships and ideas long past their expiration date, not because they are good for us, but because we're afraid of what quitting will say about us. We see quitting as a sign of weakness.

Psychologists call this the sunk cost fallacy – the tendency to keep investing in something simply because we've already put time, money or effort into it. We tell ourselves:

I've already spent five years in this job, I can't walk away now.

I've invested too much into this relationship. I have to make it work.

I already started this project, I can't quit halfway.

But here's the truth: The time you've already spent is gone and staying in something just because of past investment only leads to more wasted time.

Quit or Persevere?

Successful people quit strategically. They don't see quitting as failure – they see it as a way to redirect their energy toward something better.

Poker players fold more often than they play. They quit weak hands so they can save their resources for the hands that truly matter. Mountain climbers abandon summits if the conditions are too dangerous. They understand that getting to the top is optional, but getting back down is mandatory. Top athletes pivot when their body no longer allows them to compete. They don't see it as giving up; they see it as moving to the next phase of life.

What if quitting is the smartest, boldest and most strategic move you can make?

This is exactly the argument Annie Duke, a former professional poker player and author of *Quit*, makes: 'Quitting is not failing. Quitting is a decision – a decision to stop doing something that no longer serves you so you can free up time, energy and resources for something better.'

The question is, how do you know when to quit? It depends. Ask yourself these questions:

1. Does this align with the person I want to become?
2. Am I staying out of fear or habit rather than real desire?
3. If I were starting fresh today, would I choose this again?
4. Is continuing to invest in this stopping me from pursuing something better?

If the answers point toward quitting, then quitting isn't failure. It's wisdom.

My question for you: Is there something in your life you need to walk away from so you can say yes to something better?

KEEP EATING?

86

Time-Poor or Time-Rich?
On creating a sense of time affluence

There's an 80 per cent chance you might be time-poor. As Ashley Whillans writes in *Time Smart*, four out of five working adults report experiencing time poverty – feeling like they never have enough time. The to-do list keeps growing, work never really ends and every day feels like a race against the clock.

Time poverty increases stress, lowers productivity and diminishes our happiness. How do we escape this feeling and instead cultivate the opposite – that of time affluence or feeling like you have enough time to do what is most important to you?

Here's the surprising truth: Time poverty is often less about how much time we have and more about how we perceive and use it.

A fascinating study by Cassie Mogilner at the University of Pennsylvania shows a simple way to feel more time affluent. Mogilner and her fellow researchers took a group of university students and divided them into two groups. One group of students was told they could leave class fifteen minutes early, which gave them extra time to spend as they liked. The other group was asked to stay fifteen minutes longer and help edit essays written by underprivileged high school students.

At the end of the study, which group felt like they had more time?

Surprisingly, it was the group that gave their time away! They were more likely to feel time rich and to say they had time to spare.

Now, why would that be? Logically, it doesn't make sense. How can having less time make you feel like you have more? The students who stayed back gave time away, so they actually had less time to spare. The answer lies not in the amount of time that we spend on any given activity, but how we choose to spend our time.

As Mogilner shares, the best possible explanation is that giving your time away helps you feel more capable, confident and useful. When we do something meaningful with our time, we feel more in control of it. This sense of control expands our perception of time, making us feel like we have more of it.

Think about it: if the students had spent their extra fifteen minutes scrolling social media, would they have felt any richer in time? Likely not. Passive distractions do little to ease time scarcity and often leave us feeling more depleted.

No matter how many time-saving solutions you fill your life with, they do little to change that feeling of time poverty or scarcity if you're not using the time saved in a meaningful way. On the other hand, when you intentionally engage in rewarding and engaging activities, you feel empowered to do more with the time that you have. That is time affluence.

To create time affluence, try these mindset shifts:
1. Reframe your perception of time. Instead of saying, 'I don't have enough time,' say, 'I have all the time I need for what matters most.'
2. Engage in high-impact activities. Prioritize tasks that bring joy, purpose and meaning rather than just checking things off a list.
3. Give time away. Helping someone, mentoring or doing small acts of kindness paradoxically makes you feel like you have more time.

In the words of Seneca, 'Life, if well lived, is long enough.'

The real question isn't whether we have enough time, it's whether we are spending it in ways that truly matter.

My question to you: If you had fifteen minutes today to do something meaningful, how would you choose to spend it?

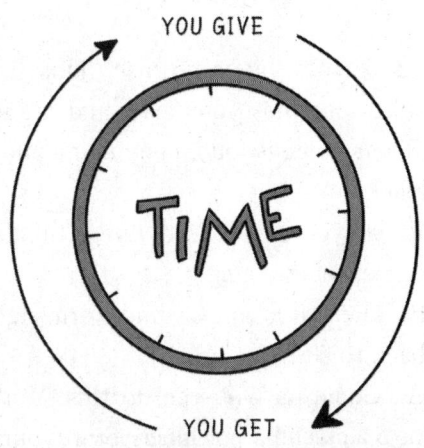

87

Inner Critic or Inner Coach?
On the two lawyers in your mind

Every day, a courtroom drama plays out in your mind. And it's just as gripping as any show you might binge-watch on Netflix, except this one shapes your life.

Inside this courtroom, there are two opposing lawyers constantly arguing their case.

Lawyer A is your greatest advocate. This lawyer believes in you, pushes you toward your goals and encourages you to take bold action. Their voice is steady, supportive and wise.

Lawyer B is your biggest critic. This lawyer feeds your self-doubt, amplifies your fears and argues for your limitations. Their voice is loud, convincing and sometimes downright cruel.

I hear both lawyers in my head. Every. Single. Day.

My alarm goes off at 5 a.m.

Lawyer B: 'The bed is so cozy and warm right now. Hit snooze. Go back to sleep!'

Lawyer A: 'Come on, you can do this. You're a proud member of the 5 a.m. club, remember? Start your day well!'

Inner Critic or Inner Coach?

I look at the hardest tasks on my to-do list.

Lawyer B: 'That looks painful. You don't need to tackle this today. Leave it for tomorrow.'

Lawyer A: 'Do it now. Get it over and done with. Then you'll have more energy for other things.'

It's time to work out.

Lawyer B: 'Skip this one. Your last workout was so intense. What difference is it going to make anyway? You are never getting that six-pack.'

Lawyer A: 'Don't focus on how you are feeling right now. Think about how you'll feel after the workout is over. And it's OK if you don't do your toughest workout today. Just show up.'

Which lawyer wins the battle in your mind? The one who is paid more. Not with money, but with your *attention*.

Know that it is a choice. You can lean in to hear the soft but firm whispers of the lawyer genuinely rooting for you, or you can let the loud and obnoxious lawyer win every single time.

As psychologist Ethan Kross, author of *Chatter*, explains: *'The voice in our head can be our greatest coach – or our worst critic. The key is learning to direct it.'*

The courtroom in your mind isn't going away. But you get to be the judge.

My question to you: Which lawyer are you going to listen to today?

272 The Conscious Choice

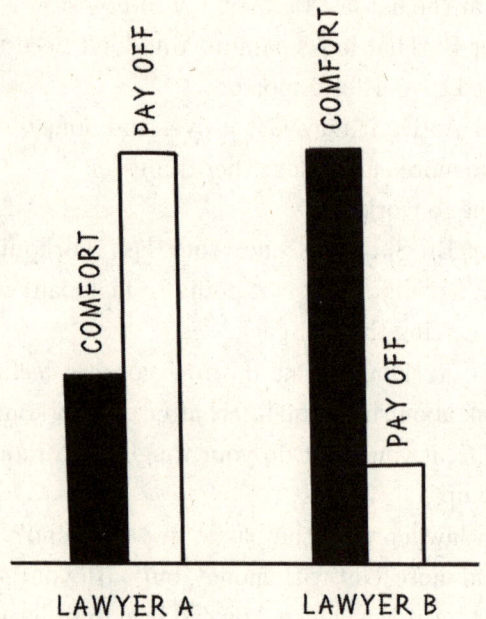

88

A Speck of Dust or a Ripple Through Time?
On the legacy we leave

If you've ever looked at a picture of Earth from space, you know how small it truly is – a tiny blue dot floating in the vastness of the universe. When you think about your individual life against that backdrop, it can feel insignificant. Almost as if nothing we do really matters in the grand scheme of things.

How much of a difference can one person really make?

I remember grappling with this question myself. Years ago, when I left the security of my corporate career to pursue something more meaningful, I wondered if my choices would have any real impact. Was I just a speck of dust, easily blown away by the winds of time?

Then, I came across a story that shifted my entire perspective:

A young man named Nipun Mehta decided to go on a walking pilgrimage across India along with his wife. They sold all their belongings in the US and bought a one-way ticket to India. They budgeted just a dollar a day for essentials and for the rest, they relied on the sheer kindness of strangers. They ate whatever food was offered to them and slept wherever they could.

When talking about what gave him the fortitude to undertake this experience during a graduation speech at the University of Pennsylvania, Nipun shared a story about his great-grandfather – an ordinary man with no wealth or prestige. Every morning, he would go on a walk and feed tiny grains of wheat to the ant hills along his path.

It was an act so small, so seemingly insignificant, that it would have been easy to dismiss. But that simple daily ritual shaped his character. It influenced his children, who then influenced their own children, setting off a ripple effect that spanned generations.

That tiny, unremarkable act was a thread in a much larger tapestry, one that would someday inspire Nipun himself to dedicate his life to service.

The ants and the ant hills are long gone. But his great-grandfather's spirit of giving lives on.

This story forever changed the way I look at our seemingly negligible lives.

Here you had a speck of dust feeding specks of dust to even tinier specks of dust and yet his impact is still being felt several generations later.

We tend to think of impact in terms of grand gestures – publishing a best-selling book, launching a billion-dollar company, changing the world in some big, visible way.

But impact rarely works like that. More often than not, it's the small, unseen choices – the way we show up for others, the kindness we extend, the encouragement we offer – that create the biggest ripples.

A Speck of Dust or a Ripple Through Time?

Yes, in the grand scheme of the universe, we are small. But that doesn't mean we are insignificant. Every action, no matter how small, sends out ripples.

Every choice you make – how you treat someone, how you show up in the world – leaves an imprint. Every moment is an opportunity to create waves that will extend far beyond what you can see.

So the question is not whether your life matters. **The question is:** What kind of ripple do you want to create?

YOU

ALSO YOU

89

Yes or No?

On the power of saying yes to life

A man once attended a meditation retreat at a Buddhist monastery. At the end of the retreat, he felt more peaceful and centered, yet something still felt missing. Before leaving, he was given the opportunity to speak with one of the monks.

He asked, 'How do you find peace?'

The monk smiled and replied, 'I say yes. To everything that happens, I say yes.'

This true story recounted by author Kamal Ravikant got me thinking. What if I were to say yes to everything? How different might this year be for me? How would my life change?

Most of our pain and suffering comes from resistance to what is. What if, instead, you surrender to all that life brings? What wisdom or gifts would you experience then?

Slowly but steadily, I have started saying yes more. Most of the time, it's a soft yes. But every now and then, I hear myself utter an active, enthusiastic *yes* and that's when I truly experience a magical shift within myself.

I work really hard at something and still don't get the results I want.

I say, 'Yes, I can learn a lesson here and do something differently, going forward.'

I go on vacation and it's raining the whole time.

I say, 'Yes, I can still make this time memorable, even if it isn't going as expected.'

I show up authentically, only to face judgment, rejection or failure.

I say, 'Yes, I can respond to this with compassion, to myself and others, despite my hurt.'

This practice of saying yes to everything is a simple yet profound way to open our hearts and minds to whatever arises in our life – opportunities and challenges as well as gifts and blessings. It allows us to work more skilfully around the resistance that we otherwise feel when our reality doesn't meet our expectations.

By saying yes, we dissolve that resistance by turning towards our fears and unpleasant emotions rather than running away. Not only does this help us feel more connected to our experiences, it unlocks a world of possibilities that only exist when we move beyond our conditioned reaction to less-than-ideal circumstances.

Here's my invitation to you: What if you were to consciously say yes to everything?

Yes to closing the gap between who you are and who you wish to be.

Yes to owning, embracing and expressing your voice in the world.

Yes to more meaningful conversations and connections.

Yes to the goals, habits and values that make you proud.
Yes to more love, more joy and more rest.
Yes to seeing the world with fresh eyes.

And finally, *yes* to whatever lessons the universe wishes to send your way. How might your life change?

Here's my question to you: What in your life would you like to say yes to?

90

Inspiration or Desperation?

On choosing the right goals

Every goal we set has an underlying motivation: it's either born out of desperation or it's ignited by inspiration.

Desperation-driven goals often stem from external pressure and expectations. They come from a place of fear, insecurity or the need for validation. They manifest as 'shoulds' – things we believe we should do to win the approval from others.

'I *should* get married by age X and have kids by age Y.'

'I *should* have a fancy job that looks great on paper.'

'I *should* live an Instagram-worthy life.'

These goals are fuelled by a sense of lack – a feeling that we are incomplete as we are. But the problem is, external validation is fleeting. Even if you achieve the goal, the sense of fulfilment is temporary. You'll soon find yourself chasing the next thing, hoping that *this* will finally bring happiness.

Psychologist Tal Ben-Shahar, in his book *Happier*, explains this as the arrival fallacy – the mistaken belief that once we achieve a certain goal, we will finally be happy.

On the other hand, goals born out of inspiration come from within. They arise from a place of passion, purpose and authenticity. They are not merely a means to an end but provide intrinsic joy and fulfilment. These goals light a fire within you – the kind of fire that makes dancers dance, writers write or leaders lead. They energize you and lift you up.

Have you ever paused to ask yourself: Am I chasing this goal out of inspiration or desperation?

When you pursue an inspired goal – a goal that makes you come alive – you do so not because you feel you are lacking, but because it resonates with your deepest self. It aligns with your values and contributes to your sense of wholeness.

Moreover, inspired goals create a powerful ripple effect. When you operate from a place of authenticity and joy, you inspire and uplift others too. Your passion and commitment serve as beacons, encouraging others to stand a little taller as they pursue their dreams and aspirations.

As social psychologist Heidi Grant Halvorson writes in *Succeed*, the goals that create more lasting happiness for us are the ones that nourish our core needs as human beings – for relatedness, competence and autonomy. Relatedness is the desire to connect with others, to feel like you belong, to love and be loved. A feeling of competence comes with any quality or skill that you are good at and allows you to meaningfully impact your environment. Finally, autonomy is the desire for freedom, to manage your time and actions as you like.

Why do we pursue goals born out of desperation? It turns out we go after superficial goals when our core needs as human beings are not met. You think to yourself, 'If I can't find the love I need, I'll get rich and famous. Then maybe I'll earn the affection and respect of others.'

Ironically, the more we go after such goals, the more we guarantee that our essential needs will *not* be met. The pursuit of socially conditioned goals takes up so much of our time and psychic energy that we don't really have time to devote to things that truly matter, such as our relationships.

The next time you set a goal, ask yourself: Am I doing this because I feel I have to? Or am I doing this because I genuinely want to?

Consciously pause to consider a goal that fills you with energy and purpose. Embrace it not as a means to an end but as a journey worth undertaking for its own sake. Remember, you are already whole, and your goals should reflect and enhance that sense of wholeness.

A question for today: What's a goal that lights a fire within you?

91

Carpe Diem or Carpe Punctum?
On seizing the moment

You've most likely heard the expression 'carpe diem'. It's Latin for 'seize the day' or more accurately, 'pluck the day'. The phrase originated in Rome almost 2,000 years ago in a collection of poems by the poet Horace.

The phrase and its philosophy have inspired countless people. In the popular movie *Dead Poets Society*, for instance, Robin Williams' character, an eccentric, textbook-ripping teacher, exclaims passionately to his eager students, 'Carpe diem. Seize the day, boys. Make your lives extraordinary!'

The idea of seizing the day sounds motivating. It conjures up intoxicating images of conquering time, knocking tasks off your to-do list, one after the other and everything going according to plan.

What's wrong with that? To begin with, a day is twenty-four hours long and seizing every hour of it can feel like a tall order. As we all know, things don't always go smoothly and we cannot control everything that happens in that time.

Carpe Diem or Carpe Punctum?

What if you have a bad morning? What if something doesn't go your way? What if someone cuts you off on your way to work, or you get an angry email from an irate colleague or client? That can often have a cascading effect on everything else and before you know it, you've written off your entire day as a terrible one. Suddenly, seizing the day then feels like a huge, uphill battle.

So, what's a better approach?

Instead of thinking of your life in years, months or even days, it is far more effective to think of your life in moments.

In his book *Everyday Enlightenment*, Dan Millman shares the expression 'carpe punctum', which means to seize the moment.

Carpe punctum is a far more empowering phrase. If the previous moment was not to your liking, you can always say, 'Yes, my morning sucked, but this – right here, right now – is a brand-new moment. How do I seize this moment? Not the entire day, but just this moment?'

You can then ask the same of the next moment and the one after that.

That is how you win the day.

There are no good days or bad days. A life is lived in moments, each one giving you an opportunity to let go of regrets from the past or worries about the future. It's about showing up as best you can in the present and being fully aware of what it requires of you.

As Eckhart Tolle reminds us, 'Realize deeply that the present moment is all you ever have. Make the Now the primary focus of your life.'

So, as you go about your day today, I won't wish you carpe diem but rather, carpe punctum.

See what happens when you turn to each moment and ask: 'How do I seize this moment? Not the entire day, but just this moment?'

CARPE DIEM

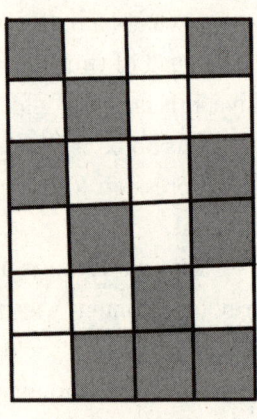

CARPE PUNCTUM

92

Jim Carrey or Percy Carrey?
On becoming the person you envision

I recently watched the documentary *Jim & Andy: The Great Beyond*, about the transformation of Jim Carrey into Andy Kaufman for the movie *Man on the Moon*. There was one particularly poignant moment that Carrey shared in the documentary that left me thinking.

Before blockbusters such as *The Mask* and *Dumb and Dumber*, before Jim Carrey became a global sensation, another Carrey played a crucial role behind the scenes – his father, Percy.

Percy Carrey wasn't a Hollywood luminary – he was a failed musician. He let go of his dream of becoming a musician to take care of his family, settling into a life of quiet resignation, sorting through tax forms as an accountant. Eventually, that ended as well. He was eventually laid off and Jim watched as his father slowly withered away.

Think about Percy for a moment. Here was a man who could've been a musician – *should've* been a musician – but found himself shuffling papers in an accounting office instead of going after his dreams. And in the end, even that job was taken from him.

Heartbreaking, you might think. Maybe. Maybe not.

This isn't a story about what Percy lost, but about what he gained and gave to his son – wisdom that is valuable for each of us. Here's what Percy told Jim: 'You can fail at what you don't want. So you might as well take a chance doing what you love.'

Jim took these words to heart and decided to give everything to his dreams. In fact, so strong was his self-belief that long before anyone even knew who he was, in 1985, Carrey made a bold decision. He wrote himself a ten million-dollar cheque for 'acting services rendered' and dated it ten years into the future.

From that day on, he carried that cheque around with him in his wallet everywhere he went. A promise to himself and an homage to his father's quiet heroism.

You may call it a coincidence but exactly ten years from that day, his dream came true when he received ten million dollars for the movie *Dumb and Dumber*. And the cheque that Jim Carrey wrote to himself? He tucked it inside the pocket of his father's pants right before Percy was buried.

Here's the thing. We often hold off on doing what we really want to because we're afraid to fail. But as Percy reminded his son – and us – you can also fail at doing what you don't want.

So the choice is yours. Do you, like Percy Carrey, take the safe path – end up doing what you don't want and risk both failure and unhappiness? Or do you, like Jim Carrey, choose to risk doing what you want and give it your all, believing it might lead to uncommon success?

My question to you: What are you choosing?
Whatever you decide, make it a conscious choice.

93

Empathy or Compassion?

On choosing the best way to support others

How do you respond to a loved one in distress? Most of us instinctively react with empathy – we feel their pain and offer words of comfort.

But what if I told you that empathy isn't always the best response? In fact, it can sometimes make things worse for both the person suffering and for you.

When the word empath first entered popular culture, it wasn't intended as something positive. In a 1956 science fiction story, 'The Empath' by J. T. McIntosh, a Scottish science fiction author, empaths were described as beings who could feel others' emotions and use this ability to exploit them.

Since then, however, empathy has taken on a largely positive connotation, often associated with deep emotional connection and kindness. It is widely touted as a virtue we should all strive for.

Yet, empathy can come at a cost. When you deeply feel another's pain, you increase your own emotional burden. If

Empathy or Compassion?

a friend is sad, you become sad. If a colleague is anxious, you absorb their anxiety. Over time, carrying the weight of other people's suffering can be exhausting.

Further, as psychologist Paul Bloom notes, while empathy may offer comfort in the short term, it is not always the most helpful response. A loved one who repeatedly makes poor life choices, for example, may need more than reassurance – they may need honest feedback and support to help them make better decisions.

What's a healthier emotion? Move from empathy to compassion.

Empathy is putting yourself in someone else's shoes. It is to look at someone who is suffering and say, 'I feel what you feel. I feel bad.' Compassion, on the other hand, is the desire to alleviate or end someone's suffering. It takes empathy a step further by asking, *'I feel what you feel. How can I help?'*

Where empathy immerses you in another's emotions, compassion empowers you to take action. That action might be as tangible as offering direct support or as simple as holding a genuine wish for their well-being.

Because compassion shifts you into a more resourceful state, it has been scientifically proven to enhance well-being. Studies show that when you feel compassion for another human being, your brain releases oxytocin – the same hormone that is released when you display physical affection towards a loved one. Where empathy can cause emotional fatigue, compassion supports resilience and leaves you feeling uplifted.

Here's my invitation to you: If you ever find yourself overwhelmed by another person's suffering, try transforming that emotional distress into a more empowering emotion by silently wishing them well. Here is a short compassion meditation which consists of reciting three simple statements silently in your mind whenever you think of someone in distress:

> May you be well.
> May you be at peace.
> May you be free of suffering.

You can choose to extend the same intention to all of humanity as well.

> May all be well.
> May all be at peace.
> May all be free of suffering.

Finally, you can bring this sense of compassion back to yourself – turn it inward.

> May I be well.
> May I be at peace.
> May I be free of suffering.

Personally, watching my parents age and experience health concerns has been particularly difficult. What has made a world of difference is beginning my day with a compassionate prayer, wishing them well. This practice not only gives me emotional strength but it also helps me take whatever action I can to support them.

My question to you: Whose pain are you feeling most strongly right now? How can you make a conscious choice to transform your empathy into a compassionate response that truly helps them?

COMPASSION IS EMPATHY + ACTION

94

Apples or Oranges?
On finding common ground

Have you heard the expression 'You can't compare apples and oranges'? It's often used to convey the idea that some things are so fundamentally different that attempting to compare them would be meaningless or unfair.

But is that really true?

Not only can you compare apples and oranges, but if you do, as Ozan Varol shares in *Think Like a Rocket Scientist*, you will find they are more similar than different.

Let's start with the obvious similarities: both are fruits of roughly the same size and shape. Both have a sweet and tangy taste. Both grow on trees in similar temperate and subtropical climates. You might wonder, then, why do we have this expression in the English language?

We use this phrase to dismiss any connection between two ideas, two concepts or even two people. How many times have you avoided connecting with someone because you thought, 'This person is so different from me. They work in another industry, have a different gender or a different sexual orientation.'

But just like apples and oranges, you and I are more similar than we are different.

When scientists completed the Human Genome Project, they found that at the base-pair level – the building blocks of DNA – all human beings are 99.9 per cent identical. In his book *Sapiens,* scholar Yuval Noah Harari argues that what unites us as humans is our ability to create and believe in stories combined with our capacity for cooperation. Meanwhile neuroscientist Matthew Lieberman, in *Social: Why Our Brains Are Wired To Connect*, explains that our need for connection is what makes us fundamentally human.

So how can we connect around our shared humanity, despite our apparent differences?

Allow me to share one of my favorite mindfulness tools: 'Just like me!'

Think of someone you would like to connect with, professionally or personally. Now, think of three ways in which the two of you are similar and end each sentence with the words 'just like me'. For example:

'She wishes to be successful, *just like me.*'

'She wants a better life for herself, and her family, *just like me.*'

'She must also experience pain and disappointment at times, *just like me.*'

'She ultimately wants peace and happiness, *just like me.*'

The more you practise this, the more you will realize you can find commonalities with any human being on the planet. On the surface, they may seem like an apple and you like an orange, but on a fundamental level, there's more that unites us than separates us.

Of course, we should accept, value and respect our differences. But let's also make space to connect around our common humanity.

So yes, compare apples and oranges – not to find the ways in which they are different, but to see how they are the same.

Here's the question I would like to leave you with. Think of someone who seems different than you. Now ask, 'How is this person also *just like me*?'

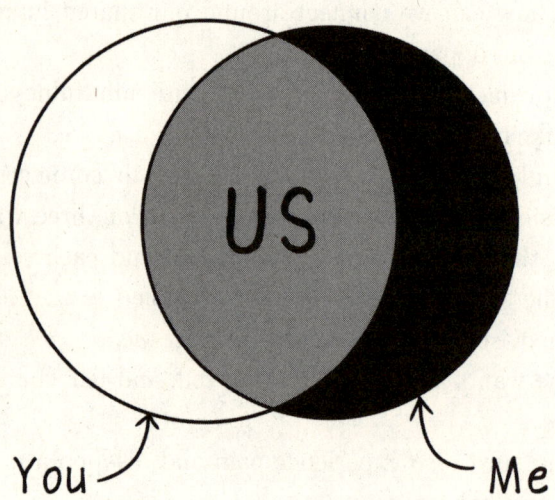

95

The Antelope or the Mouse?
On setting bold goals

A few months ago, I was contemplating applying to a PhD programme.

I casually mentioned this to my spouse. He wanted to know more, so I shared that the programme I had in mind was not from a well-known institution, but it would be entirely online and therefore easy to complete.

He looked at me confused and asked why I wouldn't consider the best programme I could find. Just as I started thinking through a few compelling reasons to offer him (or, rather, excuses!), he followed up with a statement that stopped me in my tracks:

'Bhavna, do you know the problem with setting the bar too low? It's that you *will* reach it.'

His words lingered in the air for a while, carrying a deeper truth I hadn't considered before. They reminded me of a story I'd heard once, about a lion in a jungle faced with two choices.

The lion could either go for an easy prey – the humble mouse – or set its sights on the mighty antelope. The mouse, small and seemingly powerless, would be a relatively effortless catch. But here's the thing: the energy spent in chasing the mouse would far exceed the energy gained from eating it.

On the other hand, the antelope – fast, strong and difficult to catch – would present a far greater challenge. Pursuing it would require more effort, greater speed and sheer strength. But what makes this choice truly remarkable is the promise it holds. If the lion succeeded, it could feast on the antelople for days.

In life, we often face a similar choice. We can either settle for the ordinary mouse or reach for the extraordinary antelope. The allure of an easy win and a sure path to success, is indeed strong. And so, we seek schools and programmes with guaranteed acceptance or only pursue promotions and opportunities that are well within our reach.

But here's the catch: everyone around you is chasing the same mice, which makes the competition intense. On the other hand, the antelopes are few and far between. Only the daring pursue them, simply because they demand that much more focus, effort and persistence. Yet it's precisely this scarcity that holds the key to standing out, be it in your work, your business or your life.

So, I leave you with this question: Are you chasing mice or hunting for the antelope?

The answer may just determine the heights you'll reach and the rewards you'll reap.

Choose wisely.

The Antelope or the Mouse?

96

To Seek Help or Not?
On the power of asking

In my coaching practice, I often see people struggling with the idea of asking for help – whether to request support from a colleague on a project that feels overwhelming or reach out to a potential mentor for career advice.

What keeps us from seeking help is the same thing that stops us from doing anything else where the outcome is uncertain – our mind's negativity bias. Whenever we are unsure of how something might go, our mind focuses on all that could go wrong.

You might be afraid that asking for help will come across as a sign of weakness and so – consciously or unconsciously – you train yourself to become fiercely independent. Or you may want to ask for help but fear the answer might be no and so, to protect yourself from the potential pain of rejection, you hold back.

Is there a consequence to not asking for help? Absolutely.

You feel stuck or frustrated as you keep trying to figure things out on your own. More importantly, you deprive yourself of the growth that could come from someone else's support – growth that can accelerate your career or business.

How about we change our perspective? Let's step into the shoes of the person we would like to reach out to and consider what they might experience. If you do, you will discover two things.

First, they take it as a compliment. As Dale Carnegie shares in *How to Win Friends and Influence People*, when you ask someone for a favour, you signal to them that they have something that you don't – more knowledge, more resources or more skill. It's a subtle but powerful way of showing someone genuine admiration and respect.

Second, helping you makes them feel good. When someone helps you, they experience a warm, fuzzy feeling that lifts their spirits – a feeling researchers call the 'Helper's High'. This rush of positivity occurs whenever we perform a small act of kindness for someone else. By asking for help, you give someone the opportunity to experience that feeling.

And guess what? All those good feelings then reflect positively on you since you are the one who helped induce them! This also means they are more likely to help you again in the future. A small favour can become the foundation for a stronger, lasting relationship.

The idea of building a relationship through seemingly simple requests for help is known as the Benjamin Franklin effect. The American polymath famously used this approach to win over even his most formidable adversaries. Legend has it that Franklin once asked a political rival to lend him a book. After borrowing it, he returned it with heartfelt gratitude. What began as a simple favour turned into a lifelong friendship – one that Franklin later recounted fondly in his autobiography.

The next time you hesitate to reach out to someone for support, just remember that help is one of the best things you could ask for. Not only do you get the support you need, but in seeking help, you also give the other person an opportunity to feel good about themselves. It's exactly what Shakespeare said about mercy, 'It blesseth him that gives, and him that takes'.

My question to you: Who is someone you can choose to reach out to for help today?

97

Forecast or Backcast?
On reimagining long-term goals

If you want to achieve extraordinary things in your life and career, we're told you need to think big. You need to go for moonshot goals, or BHAGs as they are called – Big, Hairy, Audacious Goals that few others even dare to imagine.

But how exactly do you dream up a better future for yourself? There are two ways – and one is better than the other.

One way is to engage in what is commonly called forecasting, where you say, 'OK, I'm now at point A in my career. If I keep going at my current rate of growth, or even a little faster, where could I realistically end up five years from today?'

Sound good?

Well, there's a problem with that. Since you are using the constraints of today to predict what will happen tomorrow, your thinking will be limited and you will hold yourself back from dreaming up an exponentially better future.

There are other problems as well. We are bad at forecasting just how much change is possible for us over a long time horizon. We assume whether it's one year from now or five years from now, we will largely remain the same – that our personality, tastes, preferences and even our values will stay stable over time.

For example, if you are risk-averse today, you might assume you will continue to have a similar level of risk-aversion five years from now.

This is what Daniel Gilbert calls the 'End of History Illusion' – the belief that we have experienced our life's worth of personal growth up to the present moment and going forward, we won't change or mature significantly.

But, as Gilbert argues in his TED Talk 'The Psychology of the Future Self', not only is change possible at any age, but we routinely underestimate just how *much* is possible.

For instance, you may continue to evolve in your ability to handle risks. To assume otherwise is to forecast your future based on faulty assumptions, which leads to poor predictions.

Not only that, as Sonja Lyubomirsky writes in *The Myths of Happiness,* another thing we fail to grasp is how surprisingly resilient we are in the face of setbacks or adversity.

We consistently overestimate how bad we will feel in the future should something go wrong and we remain cautious and conservative when assessing the challenges we are capable of taking on. That is how, instead of 'high-risk, high-reward', we often end up with 'low-risk, low reward'.

What's a better way? Don't forecast – backcast.

When backcasting, as Ozan Varol writes in *Think Like a Rocket Scientist,* you start with a blank slate. You ignore where you are today – overlook any limitations or constraints in the present – and instead, you ask,

'Where would I like to be five years from now?'

You assume that over time you can learn, grow and adapt to any circumstance and you set your vision keeping that in mind. You then reverse-engineer your way back to today to figure out what steps you need to take to realize this bold vision of yours.

This is a much better approach because it ignores the status quo of all your perceived limitations and opens up your mind to new possibilities and breakthrough ideas.

The choice is yours. You can forecast cautiously and potentially be left with regret for the life that could have been yours. Or you can backcast boldly, knowing that you can and will rise to the challenge.

Here are the questions I'd like to leave you with: What is a bold, moonshot goal that excites you? How can you backcast your way to this goal?

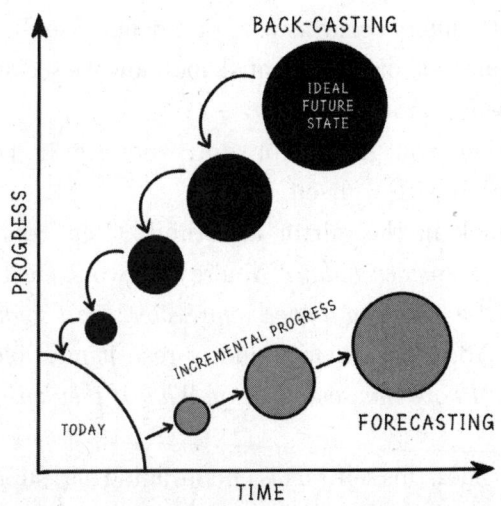

98

Encouraging or Critical?

On the conversations you have with yourself

Whom do you talk to the most? Is it your colleagues? Your children? Your spouse or partner?

The truth is, the person you talk to the most is *yourself*.

We have anywhere from 12,000 to 70,000 thoughts a day (and that number doubles on days we are feeling more anxious.) As Ethan Cross writes in his book *Chatter*, a lot of these thoughts occur as part of our inner self-talk – an ongoing internal dialogue that shapes how we see ourselves and the world around us.

Whether you like it or not, you are in constant conversation with yourself.

You look in the mirror and think, *'Ugh, what's with my bloated stomach today?'* You're at a work meeting and wonder, *'Am I making a good impression? Do I sound smart enough?'* You send an email and re-read it multiple times, thinking, *'I hope this sounds okay. What if they misinterpret it?'*

Sometimes, this self-talk is encouraging and supportive.

Other times, it can be self-critical and destructive.

Here's the thing: it's not just what happens to you that shapes your happiness and success – it's how you interpret it in your mind. You could be in the most beautiful place in the world, but if your inner dialogue is stuck on negativity, it will dull the experience. You could have just achieved something significant, but if your self-talk tells you it's *not a big deal*, your confidence won't grow.

So how do you make self-talk work *for* you instead of against you? There are two forms of self-talk you can try.

Let's say you have an important presentation coming up, with key stakeholders in the audience. Naturally, you want to make sure you do your best.

You can try what many motivational speakers swear by – engage in affirmative self-talk. You look in the mirror and pump yourself up by saying things like, 'I am the best', 'I can do this' or 'I got this'. While this form of self-talk has its benefits – and you could try this to see if it helps you – it may not work for all. For example, it may not work when you are feeling so nervous that your mind doesn't believe a word you're saying. If that's you, the good news is there is a second option that has been proven to be more effective.

It's called interrogative self-talk. Instead of forcing a statement, you turn it into a question.

Instead of saying 'I am the best,' you ask, 'How can I do my best?'

Instead of 'This is going to go well,' you ask, 'What can I do to make this go well?'

Research by Kenji Noguchi, Ibrahim Senay and Dolores Albarracín confirms that interrogative self-talk is more effective than affirmations. When you ask a question, your brain searches for answers, helping you feel more prepared and resourceful.

My questions to you: What are you telling yourself daily? And how can you transform your inner chatter into powerful questions that lead you forward?

99

Talent or Skill?

On what truly leads to success

What do you think drives the achievements of the most successful people you know, talent or skill? Take the likes of Michael Jordan, Virat Kohli or Indra Nooyi – were these individuals born with magical, innate abilities that propelled them forward, or was it the relentless cultivation of skills that lead to their greatness?

At first glance, talent and skill might seem interchangeable. But they are not the same thing.

Here's how Seth Godin describes it in *Practice*: 'Talent is something we're born with – it's in our DNA, a magical alignment of gifts. But skill? Skill is earned. It's learned and practised and hard-won.'

Here's the good news: you don't need talent to succeed. Even if you don't see yourself as naturally gifted, you can still become exceptional at anything you choose to pour your effort into.

Angela Duckworth, in her book *Grit*, breaks it down into two simple equations:

Talent × Effort = Skill
Skill × Effort = Achievement

Her insight is simple but profound: effort counts twice. If you take talent and apply effort, you develop a skill. If you take that skill and keep applying effort toward a goal, you achieve excellence.

It's not about being *born* with something. It's about *building* it over time.

If talent alone guaranteed success, Michael Jordan wouldn't have gone onto become the icon that he became.

Because here's something most people don't know: Jordan was cut from his high school basketball team.

As a sophomore, he tried out for the varsity squad and was rejected for being too short. A setback like this could have ended his career before it even began. But instead of accepting this as a sign that he wasn't talented enough, Jordan used it as fuel to work harder than anyone else.

He practised relentlessly. He would wake up at 5 a.m. to train before school. He spent hours perfecting his jump shot, dribbling and defence. He conditioned his body, eventually growing taller, stronger and faster.

His effort turned talent into mastery.

Years later, when asked about his success, Jordan didn't talk about natural ability. He talked about hard work. 'I have failed over and over and over again in my life. And that is why I succeed.'

This same principle applies to every area of life.

If you want to be a great speaker, you don't have to be *born* with charisma. You just have to practise.

If you want to write a book, you don't need a natural gift with words. You just need to write consistently.

If you want to lead a team, you don't have to be *born* a leader. You just have to learn, adapt and grow.

The questions I leave you with are: What's one skill you want to develop? How much effort are you willing to put in to make it happen?

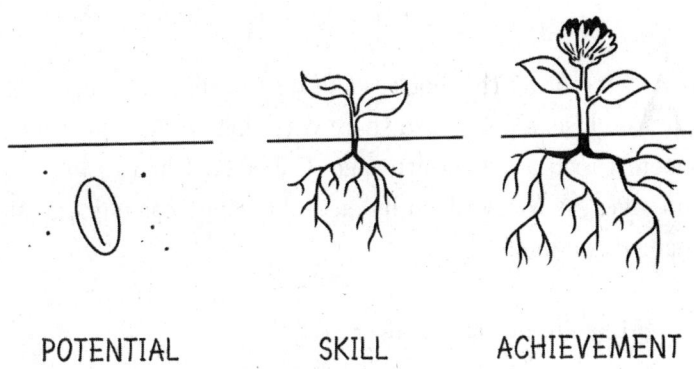

POTENTIAL   SKILL   ACHIEVEMENT

100

Start or Restart?
On the power of fresh beginnings

As we bring this book – and our journey together – to a close, allow me to share with you an excerpt from a poem I read a few months ago. Called 'If I had to live my life over', it was written by an eighty-five-year-old woman named Nadine Stair.

> If I had to live my life over...
>
> I'd dare to make more mistakes next time.
> I'd relax. I would limber up.
> I would be sillier than I have been this trip.
> I would take fewer things seriously ...
>
> Oh, I've had my moments and if I had it to do over again,
> I'd have more of them.
> In fact, I'd try to have nothing else.
> Just moments
> one after another,
> instead of living so many years ahead of each day.

Start or Restart?

This poem really got me thinking ... how would I live my life over? How would *you* live your life over?

What would you do less of and what would you do more of?

Would you care less about what other people think? Worry less about what might happen? Stress less about imaginary demons?

Would you instead laugh more? Dance more? Follow your heart more?

And then I felt a wave of gratitude rush over me, because I realized I don't have to live my life over. I have, I hope, many precious years left, as do you.

You don't need to wait until you're older to face the realization that you wish you had done things differently. A better question to ask then is: How would you like to spend the precious years that you have left?

Psychology tells us you can leverage the 'fresh start' effect – a psychological phenomenon where individuals are more likely to pursue goals or make significant changes in their behaviour after temporal landmarks that represent new beginnings. It could be the start of a new week, month, year or even a personal event like a birthday or holiday.

Reaching the end of this book could be that temporal landmark for you. Use this day to renew your commitment to live a life that's more aligned with what is most important to you. And make a fresh start!

Remember, you are just one conscious choice away from a completely different life.

My final question to you: If you were to make a fresh start today, what would your first conscious choice be?

Acknowledgements

Writing this book has been a journey of reflection, growth and deep gratitude. There are so many people who have shaped my path and made this work possible, and I am profoundly thankful for each of you.

To my darling husband, Anshumani, my unwavering pillar of strength – your encouragement, belief in me and steadfast support have carried me through every step of this journey. To my darling son, Ahvaan, the purest source of joy in my life – you remind me every day of the beauty of curiosity, play and wonder.

To my parents, whose love, sacrifices and values have shaped the person I am today – this book, in many ways, is a testament to the lessons you have instilled in me. To my siblings, Dev and Mona, whom I cherish deeply – your presence in my life is a gift and I am grateful for our bond.

To my wider extended family, including my dearest in-laws, thank you for believing in me. To each of you, individually and collectively, the expression that captures what you mean to me is the African philosophy of Ubuntu: '*I am because we are.*'

To my Shenomics community, you are my constant source of inspiration. Each day you remind me why this work matters. Your courage, commitment and passion fuel my own. To my core team – Sreelakshmi, Charu, and Puja – this mission would not be possible without you. Your dedication and belief in the power of conscious leadership make everything we do at Shenomics come alive.

To the mentors and teachers who have guided me over the years – thank you for challenging me, expanding my perspective and showing me the way. Your wisdom has been invaluable in shaping my journey and deepening my commitment to a life of service.

I also want to thank key individuals without whose support this book would not have come to life. Beginning with my agent, Mita, who has been instrumental in bringing this dream of mine to reality. A special thank you to Meghna, the illustrator for the book, who has beautifully captured the essence of each chapter in a thought-provoking yet fun way.

A huge thank you to the entire team at Pan Macmillan India – Pujitha, for her leadership; Shreyoshee, for her meticulous attention to detail in the edits; Saburi, for her marketing vision and support; Suhail, for his invaluable sales expertise; and Bazila, for her diligent proofreading. It truly takes a village to bring a book to life and I could not be more grateful for the incredible tribe behind mine.

This book exists because of each of you. Thank you for being part of this journey.

Bibliography

Bryan, C. J., Allison Master, and G. M. Walton. "'Helping' versus 'being a helper': Invoking the self to increase helping in young children". *Child Development*, 85(5), 1836–1842 (2014). https://doi.org/10.1111/cdev.12244

Chambliss, Catherine, Ashley Cattai, Peter Benton et al. "Freudenfreude and Schadenfreude Test (FAST) Scores of Depressed and Non-Depressed Undergraduates". *Psychological Reports*, 111(1), 115–116 (2012). https://doi.org/10.2466/02.07.21.PR0.111.4.115-116

Chase, C.C., D. B. Chin, M. A. Oppezzo et al. "Teachable Agents and the Protégé Effect: Increasing the Effort Towards Learning". *Journal of Science Education and Technology*, 18, 334–352 (2009). https://doi.org/10.1007/s10956-009-9180-4

Christakis, N. A. and Fowler, J. H. "The spread of obesity in a large social network over 32 years". *The New England Journal of Medicine*, 357(4), 370–379 (2007). https://doi.org/10.1056/NEJMsa066082

College of Continuing & Professional Studies, University of Minnesota; "Building High-Performing Teams: 8

Strategies for Successful Team Development"; https://ccaps.umn.edu/story/building-high-performing-teams-8-strategies-successful-team-development

de Berker, A. O., R. B. Rutledge, Christoph Mathys et al. "Computations of uncertainty mediate acute stress responses in humans". *Nature Communications*, 7, 10996 (2016). https://doi.org/10.1038/ncomms10996

Depow, G. J., Zoë Francis, and Michael Inzlicht. "The Experience of Empathy in Everyday Life". *Psychological Science*, 32(8), 1198–1213 (2021). https://doi.org/10.1177/0956797621995202

Fredrickson, B. L. and Christine Branigan. "Positive emotions broaden the scope of attention and thought-action repertoires". *Cognition and Emotion*, 19(3), 313–332 (2011). https://doi.org/10.1080/02699930441000238

Google re:Work; "Understand team effectiveness"; https://rework.withgoogle.com/en/guides/understanding-team-effectiveness

Institute on Character; "The 24 Character Strengths"; https://www.viacharacter.org/character-strengths

KPMG; "Mind the Gap"; https://assets.kpmg.com/content/dam/kpmg/xx/pdf/2022/12/mind-the-gap.pdf

Lin, I. M., Tai, L. Y., and Fan, S. Y. "Breathing at a rate of 5.5 breaths per minute with equal inhalation-to-exhalation ratio increases heart rate variability". *International Journal of Psychophysiology*, 91(3), 206–211 (2014). https://doi.org/10.1016/j.ijpsycho.2013.12.006

Lyubomirsky, Sonja and Kristin Layous. "How Do Simple Positive Activities Increase Well-Being?". *Current Directions in Psychological Science*, 22(1), 57–62 (2013). https://doi.org/10.1177/0963721412469809

Massey, G.R. and Elias Kyriazis. "Interpersonal trust between marketing and R&D during new product development projects". *European Journal of Marketing*, 41(9/10), 1146–1172 (2007). https://doi.org/10.1108/03090560710773381

McGonigal, Kelly. "Mindfulness and Weight Loss". Idea Health & Fitness Association. https://www.ideafit.com/ampmindfulness-weight-loss/

Mogilner, Cassie. "You'll Feel Less Rushed If You Give Time Away". Harvard Business Review. https://hbr.org/2012/09/youll-feel-less-rushed-if-you-give-time-away

Mogilner, Cassie, Zoë Chance, and M. I. Norton. "Giving Time Gives You Time". *Psychological Science*, 23(10), 1233–1238 (2012). https://doi.org/10.1177/0956797612442551

Noble, D. J. and Shawn Hochman. "Hypothesis: Pulmonary Afferent Activity Patterns During Slow, Deep Breathing Contribute to the Neural Induction of Physiological Relaxation". *Frontiers in Physiology*, 10, 1176 (2019). https://doi.org/10.3389/fphys.2019.01176

Patrick, V. M. and Henrik Hagtvedt. ""I Don't" versus "I Can't": When Empowered Refusal Motivates Goal-Directed Behavior". *Journal of Consumer Research*, 39(2), 371–381 (2012). https://doi.org/10.1086/663212

Pychyl, T. A. and G. L. Flett. "Procrastination and Self-Regulatory Failure: An Introduction to the Special Issue." *Journal of Rational-Emotive & Cognitive-Behavior Therapy*, 30, 203–212 (2012). http://dx.doi.org/10.1007/s10942-012-0149-5

Rafaeli, Eshkol and M. E. J. Gleason. "Skilled support within intimate relationships". *Journal of Family Theory & Review*. 1(1), 20–37 (2009). https://doi.org/10.1111/j.1756-2589.2009.00003.x

Reill, Amanda. "A Simple Way to Make Better Decisions". Harvard Business Review. https://hbr.org/2023/12/a-simple-way-to-make-better-decisions

Segar, Michelle, J. M. Taber, Heather Patrick et al. "Rethinking physical activity communication: using focus groups to understand women's goals, values, and beliefs to improve public health". *BMC Public Health*, 17, 462 (2017). https://doi.org/10.1186/s12889-017-4361-1

Senay, Ibrahim, Dolores Albarracín, and Kenji Noguchi. "Motivating Goal-Directed Behavior Through Introspective Self-Talk: The Role of the Interrogative Form of Simple Future Tense." *Psychological Science*, 21(4), 499–504 (2010). https://doi.org/10.1177/0956797610364751

Simmons, Rachel and Herminia Ibarra. "Career Sponsorship Is a Two-Way Street". Harvard Business Review. https://hbr.org/2023/02/career-sponsorship-is-a-two-way-street

Sturgeon J. A. and A. J. Zautra. "Social pain and physical pain: shared paths to resilience". *Pain* Management,

6(1), 63–74 (2016). https://doi.org/10.2217/pmt.15.56

Summerville, Amy and N. J. Roese. "Dare to Compare: Fact-Based versus Simulation-Based Comparison in Daily Life". *Journal of Experimental Social Psychology*, 44(3), 664–671 (2008). https://doi.org/10.1016/j.jesp.2007.04.00220.

Westgate, E. C. "Why Boredom Is Interesting". *Current Directions in Psychological Science*, 29(1), 33–40 (2019). https://doi.org/10.1177/0963721419884309

Wilson, T. D., D. A. Reinhard, E. C. Westgate et al. "Just think: the challenges of the disengaged mind". *Science*, 345(6192), 75–7 (2014). https://doi.org/10.1126/science.1250830

Yeager, D. S., Valerie Purdie-Vaughns, Julio Garcia et al. "Breaking the cycle of mistrust: wise interventions to provide critical feedback across the racial divide". *Journal of Experimental Psychology: General*. 143(2), 804–24 (2014).